The New Anointing

By

Morris Cerullo

Dealing with the problems and
circumstances in your life
through a revelation of the
ROOT CAUSE, you can have a
New Anointing for **total victory!**

Published by
Morris Cerullo World Evangelism
San Diego, California

1st printing 1975
2nd printing 1976
3rd printing 1978
4th printing 1980
5th printing 1983
6th printing 1988
7th printing 1999
8th printing 2002
9th printing 2003

Over 250,000 copies in print

My personal promise to you...

Jesus said, "The spirit of the Lord GOD is upon me: because the LORD hath anointed me to preach good tidings unto the meek; he hath sent me to bind up the brokenhearted, to proclaim liberty to the captives, and the opening of the prison to them that are bound..."

(Isaiah 61:1)

There was a divine anointing on Jesus that gave Him God's **power** to cause the blind to see, the deaf to hear, the lame to walk, to deliver the demon-possessed and raise the dead.

This same anointing can be yours...I call it the **New Anointing** because it has been lost, even ignored, by the Church in our time.

There is a secret to overcoming your problems, failures, temptations, circumstances and unanswered prayers. Once you receive this revelation and learn that your problems are not caused by circumstances, people, ideologies or things, but by spiritual forces behind the scenes...you will have discovered the ROOT CAUSE to your problems...you will know how to deal with them...and you will know how to live in complete victory!

As you learn the keys to the New Anointing you will deal a fatal blow to Satan and his demonic forces which are hindering your life, your family and your ministry.

Morris Cerullo

IS THERE A DEVIL...
IS SATAN REAL?

BILLY GRAHAM SAYS:

"All of us engaged in Christian work are constantly aware of the fact that we have to do battle with supernatural forces and powers. The devil follows me every day. He tempts me. He is a very real presence to me."

In a recent article in the *National Enquirer,* Billy Graham is quoted as saying:

"There is a connection between the devil and the increase of drugs, pornography, sexual license, and the occult in the U.S. We see people who are committing all kinds of violence, mass murders, and we have learned they have been involved with the occult. The very word 'witchcraft' stems from the same Greek word as the word 'drugs.' "

POPE PAUL VI SAYS:

"The smoke of Satan has entered the Temple of God through a fissure in the Church...

"Evil is not merely a lack of something—but an effective agent— a living, spiritual being—a terrible reality, mysterious and frightening."

EVAN ROBERTS, LEADER OF THE GREAT WELSH REVIVAL, SAYS:

"The devil's great purpose, for which he fights, is to keep the world in ignorance of himself, his ways, and his colleagues: and the Church is taking sides with him when siding with ignorance about him."

MORRIS CERULLO

"I believe that special evil sinister forces of Satan have been assigned the devilish task of destroying the structure and society of this nation."

April, 1970, Denver Hilton Hotel, Deeper Life Conference

GOD SAID:

"God said to me, 'Son, I am going to send a New Anointing of My divine healing power to North America.' "

Island of Grenada, January, 1964, Morris Cerullo

TABLE OF CONTENTS

Chapter 1—Look Over My Shoulder 3

Chapter 2—Is It Too Late? 9

Chapter 3—Revelation Is Exciting 19

Chapter 4—A Vision Of The Rapture 27

Chapter 5—A Call To Arms 35

Chapter 6—Entering The Flow Of God's Power . . . 43

Chapter 7—The Charismatic Revival And You! 55

Chapter 8—The Missing Link 69

Chapter 9—Locating Your Enemy 83

Chapter 10—A Sense Of Purpose 97

Chapter 11—How To Move From Imitation To
            Participation 113

Chapter 12—A Cloud Of Witnesses 125

PREFACE

God has given me the wonderful privilege of personally training more than 500,000 ministers and workers around the world during the past forty years.

When I say training, I do not mean the normal basic theological training of the seminary. I am speaking of going one step further than the fundamentals of how to prepare and deliver a good message—I am speaking of training that motivates men and women to go beyond the normal, to enable them to work the works of God.

Numbers are not everything. God is more interested in quality than quantity, and by that I mean spiritual capability. At the same time, I also know that He is *"not willing that any should perish" (II Peter 3:9)*. Therefore, if the same approaches and tools can win 10,000 souls to Christ instead of 10, we are responsible for using them.

Our message to Nationals around the world for the past forty years has been this: "You can see the same results in your ministry as you are seeing in our crusades if you will simply step out in faith and follow the biblical pattern."

I believe firmly that there are "keys to the kingdom." Whenever God gives us a special commission to do a special work, I know that He will provide the keys that will unlock the door to effective ministry. We will not be grinding in the same rut that has been worn deeper and deeper over the years to produce less and less fruit for the kingdom of God.

Years ago, God commanded us to return to America for meetings. I chafed under this because of the tremendous success God was giving to us on the foreign missionary fields. At the same time, I knew that God would have to

1

provide a key that would open up our cities for the Gospel.

If the Lord were to tell us everything at once, as He leads us through this life, it would overwhelm us! When I look back on the development of this revelation in my ministry, I can see so clearly the step-by-step process the Holy Spirit used to bring this revelation to my heart; and the most beautiful thing is that it is still coming account of the Holy Spirit perfecting that key of the miracle anointing that is applicable on both the individual and the national level.

God wants the overcoming life to be in you first that you might launch out to affect your neighborhood, your community, your state, your province, and your nation for the kingdom of our Lord.

A lady recently commented at one of our Schools of Ministry, "You sit in the morning and are so blessed by this revelation and what it can do. Then in the afternoon the Lord gives you the opportunity to put it to work."

What she is saying is that you had better be prepared to put it into action. It will be very difficult for you to read this book and not immediately begin to put it to use, and God will give you the opportunity.

As you begin a wonderful, exciting journey into the spirit of the revelation of the New Anointing, I want to promise you two things.

ONE: Your life will never be the same. Something marvelous will happen to you, as the Holy Spirit takes you on into the Presence of God in a new and fresh way.

TWO: You will enter into prayer victories never before experienced—and doors to the kingdom of heaven and all of its blessings will become much more of a reality to you! You will find yourself over and over again putting that key into heaven's door and pressing through to a NEW experience of prayer power that will bring you prayer victories never before experienced.

Chapter 1

LOOK OVER MY SHOULDER

Today is one of those rare occasions when I am sitting at my desk here in the home office in San Diego, California.

When I am here, the greatest portion of my time is spent reading and personally answering correspondence and in intercessory prayer for the special prayer requests which are sent to us.

I want you to come around to my side of the desk for a moment and look over my shoulder; I won't show you the names because they are held in strict confidence, but I do want to share with you some of the needs of our precious friends. Maybe you will see one of these letters and say, "Brother Cerullo, I could have written that letter. I have that same problem."

Before we read the first letter, let me tell you that in all of our ministry we have never experienced such a flood of letters testifying of real victories and miracles, most of which have resulted from either reading or hearing the revelation of the New Anointing.

Still, there are those who have not yet grasped the

revelation to the point where they have become more than conquerors. . . .

THIS GENERATION

Look at this letter from the mother of a teenage daughter:

"Brother Cerullo, we are members of a traditional church and have always taken our children to Sunday school. Our daughter was a good girl and was always active in the various church activities, until about a year ago when her attitude started to change. She became very disrespectful of both her father and me, and was very evasive when we would ask her where she was going at night.

"I found out last night that she has obtained birth control pills from a public health agency. I know now that she is using drugs with increasing frequency. Both her father and I have tried to reason with her. I have prayed for her, but she only seems to be getting further and further away from us. I fear at any moment she will leave home and we will never see her again. What can I do?"

BROKEN FAMILIES

And, listen to this young wife:

"Brother Cerullo, I met my husband in church, we were both Spirit-filled believers and very active in church work. This continued after we were married and through the birth of our two wonderful children. We were happy and very much in love, but about six months ago, something strange came over him and he just wasn't the same man that I married. He came home last night and said that he is in love with someone else and wants a divorce. I cried all night long; it seems my world has come to an end. Is there any answer?"

BOUND BY HABITS

Another is bound by the tobacco habit:

"Brother Cerullo, I have been a Christian for three years. It has been the most glorious period of my life. I have seen many wonderful prayer victories, but I am bound by the cigarette habit, and I have done everything I know how, but I cannot get free. When I go to buy cigarettes, I feel so embarrassed and so bad that I actually cry—but I cannot help myself. Can you help me?"

THOUGHT CONTROL

Here is a case that is probably the most common cause of a powerless Christian life:

"Brother Cerullo, I am really ashamed to reveal what I am about to write, and unless you can give me some answers, I feel that my Christian life is in jeopardy. I have a wonderful wife and three lovely children. I attend church regularly and even teach Sunday school—but no one, not even my family, knows the turmoil inside of me. I cannot get control of my thought life. The most evil imaginations come into my mind. I fight them, but feel powerless to cast them out. I will wake up in the middle of the night with visions of the most immoral things. I have done everything I know. I have prayed, I have fasted, but it is only getting worse. What can I do?''

PASTOR'S PROBLEMS

There are more pastors leaving the ministry than ever before. Here is a typical reason:

"Brother Cerullo, I have been a successful pastor for the past fifteen years, and at the moment we have a lovely church and everything on the outside appears to be just beautiful. On the inside it is a different story. I am at the end of my rope. I don't see anything happening in the spiritual lives of my people. I preach about dedication and holiness and most of our congregation has received the Baptism of the Holy Spirit. The trouble is that I cannot find any fruit of the Spirit. For a midweek dinner we can have a crowd, but for a prayer meeting there is only a handful. Brother Cerullo, I am tired of playing church and unless something happens, I am going to seek a secular position. Money is not my motive, but I cannot take the frustration any longer of preaching my heart out and seeing nothing happen. What would you advise me to do?''

LOST AUTHORITY

A mother who had lost control:

"Brother Cerullo, please pray for my children. I cannot understand their rebellious attitude and lack of respect for their mother and father. We have brought them up in church and Sunday school, but in the last six months there has been a total disintegration of authority in our house. They don't feel that I have the right to tell them when they should come in at night or when they cannot go out. The oldest one is fourteen and they still all attend church, but I see no Christian attitudes in them whatsoever. I have tried everything I know how to do, but it is only getting worse. Please help me!"

UNCONTROLLABLE SPIRIT

Does this sound like you?

"Brother Cerullo, I don't know if you can help me, but there is something that is keeping me from the victory that Christ has for my life. I have an uncontrollable temper. What I can't understand is that I will absolutely blow up over the silliest things and afterward I can't really believe that I could allow such little things to bother me. Just when I seem to be gaining ground in my Christian life, some little irritant will cause me to say the most cutting, destructive things to those that I love. Each time it seems to be getting worse and it is to the point now that I am actually afraid that I will do some violent thing that even time will not repair. I am desperate."

APPETITES

Is there a spirit of gluttony?

"Brother Cerullo, that Scripture that speaks of those whose God is their belly is tormenting me day and night because I cannot help but eat everything I can get my hands on. I know that physically I am destroying myself, but worse is the havoc that is in my spiritual life. I love God, I read my Bible, I pray, others have prayed and are praying for me, but I just can't quit. I have tried to fast, but the pain and craving was too much for me. Brother Cerullo, I know that I can never please God, and I really feel that unless I find deliverance my soul shall perish as well. It took me a long time before I could bring myself around to write you this letter, and I hope you can help me."

We could go on and on through this stack of letters before me, but in essence they would all be the same. They tell me story after story of heartbreak and trouble, with no help in sight.

Is there an answer for them? What can I tell them? Where can they find real help?

Chapter 2

IS IT TOO LATE?

THE TRUE TEST OF A PROPHET IS THAT WHAT HE SPEAKS WILL COME TO PASS

Several years ago I made the claim that the pornography, loose morals, dope problem, illicit sex, homosexuality, rioting in the streets of the world by young people, drug addicts, and revolutionaries, were a result of more than just the changing times we live in; they are more than just the result of young people disenchanted with the so-called hypocrisy of the older generation or a new set of morals coming upon the world.

There is a war in the unseen world being waged, and its commander in chief is Satan.

The devil was the first misfortune of mankind. He was the cunning originator of the original sin. From the fall of Adam, the devil acquired dominion over man, which only the redemption power of Christ can save us from.

Satan is Enemy Number One—and he still acts with treacherous cunning. He is the unseen enemy who sows destruction, death, suffering, and all evil in human

9

history. The Bible says, *"The thief cometh not, but for to steal, and to kill, and to destroy." (John 10:10)*

On the other side of the coin is the great news that we know how to deal with Satan. The Bible is our training manual.

You cannot fight an enemy that you are blinded to. You cannot fight an enemy that you cannot locate or of whom you have no knowledge of his strength. That is why Jesus said, *"Ye shall know the truth, and the truth shall make you free!" (John 8:32)*

I FOUND THAT THERE WERE NO DIFFERENCES BETWEEN CIVILIZED AND UNCIVILIZED NATIONS

For years my own eyes were blinded to what was happening in the civilized world.

I recognized the unseen forces of Satan on the mission fields.

I engaged them in spiritual battle for hours in my hotel room day after day as I prepared to stand before the thousands of people who came to the stadiums and fields in foreign crusades on the mission fields from Asia to Africa to South America.

Evan Roberts, the great Welsh revivalist, said:

If missionaries to the heathen recognized the existence of evil spirits, and that the darkness in heathen lands was caused by the prince of the power of the air... *"For we wrestle not against flesh and blood, but against principalities, against powers, against rulers of the darkness of this world, against spiritual wickedness in high places." (Ephesians 6:12)*

"Having the understanding darkened, being alienated from the life of God through the ignorance that is in them, because of the blindess of their heart." (Ephesians 4:18)

"And we know that we are of God, and the whole world lieth in wickedness." (I John 5:19)

"In whom the god of this world hath blinded the minds of them which believe not, lest the light of the glorious gospel of Christ, who is the image of God, should shine unto them." (II Corinthians 4:4)

...and proclaimed to the heathen the message of deliverance from the evil hosts as well as the remission of sin and victory over sin through the atoning sacrifice of Calvary—a vast change would come over the mission field in a few brief years.

(Evan Roberts From *War on The Saints*)

This is exactly what we have done for years on the great mission fields of the world with the result that thousands have come to Christ.

I never thought that in civilized, intelligent, educated America, Canada, England and Europe that this demon power on the loose among the masses was the real problem.

I attributed the decline in Christianity and church attendance to increased affluence, TV, movies and sexual promiscuousness.

A SINISTER PLOT

Little did I realize that what was happening in North America, Europe and around the world was a sinister plot of Satan to unleash his forces (even to the bewilderment and blindness of the Church) upon our society.

Now only a call to battle by the Church can stop him!

We have been bringing our sons and daughters to Christ—telling them that if they just come to Jesus, everything will be all right and everything will work out fine. Oh, the disillusionment that has been the result!

Nothing could be further from the truth.

We have trained them as Sons of God! But we have forgotten that the call to Christ is a call to spiritual battle, and consequently we have not trained them to be soldiers.

The evidence that this is true is the untold loss

of multitudes of young people from the Church and from any involvement whatsoever in the things of God.

Further evidence of this truth is the tremendous number of children of saved parents who have rebelled against the faith of their mothers and fathers, while the parents stood and watched helplessly crying, "Oh, God, where did we fail You? What did we do wrong that caused our child to wander out into the world?"

The truth is that the call of Jesus is a **call to battle**.

NOT READY FOR BATTLE

We have not prepared soldiers!

(1) We have not given them information on the enemy!
(2) We have not revealed who the devil really is, and the great evil he is capable of.
(3) We, as parents, have not prepared our sons and daughters for spiritual battle; neither has the Church of God prepared "God's sons" for this battle.

For years I sat in this vortex of spiritual bewilderment wondering just what it would take to unleash harvest in North America.

One day God spoke to me in a small hotel room where I was fasting and praying in Madras, India. He gave me the answer:

"Son, the sooner you realize you are not dealing with men, or with political ideologies, or with things (drugs, disenchanted young people, homosexuality, cancer, arthritis, tumors, high and low blood pressure, sugar conditions in the blood), but that you are dealing with spirits and are in a spiritual conflict to deliver My people, the sooner you will have the victory for My people!"

"For we wrestle not against flesh and blood, but against principalities, against powers, against the rulers of the darkness of this world, against spiritual wickedness in high places." (Ephesians 6:12)

Here was the answer as plain as the nose on my face. Going back to the early Church I began to understand:

(1) They recognized the existence of evil spirits.
(2) They knew that evil spirits deceived and possessed men.
(3) They understood that the devil was out to hurt, kill, and destroy mankind.
(4) And they knew that Christ gave His followers authority over the devil and evil spirits through His Name!

The Church of Jesus Christ today, as in the days of its beginning, must lay hold on the equipment of the apostolic period for dealing with the influx of the evil among her members if the Church is to survive!

This is what the revelation of the New Anointing is all about.

HISTORY'S GREATEST CHALLENGE

The Church and the individual Christian has a greater challenge today than at any time in history. In God's dealing with Israel and in the history of the Church, the point of greatest crisis brought forth the greatest manifestation of the power of God.

Man had to seek God for it. It did not come automatically! When Israel began to pray and to seek the face of God, a revelation came that restored the power, that restored the vitality to the spiritual life of the individual and the nation—but man had to seek it. Man must sincerely desire to know and possess this power in order to receive it. As the Bible says, *"Ask, and it shall be given you." (Luke 11:9)*

This chapter asks the question, "Is it too late?"

The answer is an unequivocal no!

It is not too late, and we have every reason to believe that God has sent us the answer. Be careful though, God's answers are not always easy to accept, and sometimes they demand tremendous dedication of our lives—but one of the greatest secrets I have learned through times of great trial and decision is to always trust the Holy Spirit. What may at the moment appear difficult, may be the very doorway into the most beautiful experience and blessing of your life.

You are approaching that doorway right now!

Don't be afraid to step through it.

Victory and power in every area of your life await you on the other side.

We have made a spiritual breakthrough!

WILL AMERICA BE HEALED?

Even as *TIME Magazine* said, with the inauguration of President Ford in 1974, "THE HEALING BEGINS." President Ford often said that he wanted "to bind up the nation's wounds."

How closely these words parallel the words of Jesus, in *Isaiah 61*, where He said, *"The Spirit of the Lord God is upon me; because the Lord hath anointed me to preach good tidings unto the meek; he hath sent me to bind up the brokenhearted..."*

To bind up the nation's wounds!

We believe that a national healing of North America will take place...and that healing is what we have prophesied in this ministry for many years. A New Anointing that God promised He would send is coming to North America.

This is the New Anointing we are talking about. A national revival of unprecedented scale which will shake North America to the very foundations and rebuild it spiritually from the bottom up.

We have a new vision of what God will do in North America—and we expect it to come to pass. That is why we called this breakthrough in the Spirit a revelation. We know what will happen in North America. God is going to use North America as never before to reach the unsaved millions around the world.

That does not mean there will not be trouble. There will be. There will be distress of nations, and perplexity as never before. But the light of Jesus Christ, before the end of the age, shall arise and shine, and the glory of the Lord shall rise over North America as never before.

God has given me a prayer for North America. By faith I want you to join me in this prayer! Place your hand right now on this book as our point of agreement. God says, *"If two of you shall agree on earth as touching any thing that they shall ask, it shall be done for them of my Father which is in heaven." (Matthew 18:19)*

Let us pray right now! Read the prayer in a spirit of intercession and faith. This is not ritual or form. God will hear us now as we together pray this prayer in the Name of Jesus!

A PRAYER FOR AMERICA

Let us pray: "Father, we bring to You this great nation of ours, this nation that was born and conceived in liberty; this nation that was born and conceived upon the principles of God; this nation that received its constitution not from the philosophy of man, not adopted from some heathen nation, but this great nation, my God, that received its constitution from You as men sought You in the wee hours of the morning, as men prayed for a constitution that could lead a country, that could lead a people, that could establish a nation, not upon the philosophy of man, but that could establish a nation upon the principles of Almighty God.

"Father, in the Name of Jesus, we pray for our country right now.

"We pray that You will send a spirit of conviction out over this great nation.

"We pray, God that You will loose the Holy Spirit, that He will convict the leaders of this nation.

"God, there is sin, much sin, in the camps; not only what we have read in the papers but those things which are hid in the inner workings or the depths.

"God, we are not talking about Republicans, or Democrats, or Independents. God, we are talking about men, men who need to have holiness as the characteristic of their lives, who need to have integrity and honesty as the very basic characteristics of their beings.

"We pray, oh God, that You will send out a spirit of healing over this nation.

"We pray, oh God, that you will release the New Anointing upon this nation.

"We pray that it will come upon the leaders of the land.

"God, we pray in the Name of Jesus that there shall be a crying in the middle of the night.

"We pray, God, that leaders shall get out of their beds and shall drop to their knees and shall repent before Thee, realizing that the power that is placed in their hands is a tremendous responsibility of leadership to govern, to guide, to direct the masses of humanity.

"Oh God, this nation does not belong to Satan, it does not belong to pornography, it does not belong to loose morals, it does not belong to the elimination of prayer and Bible reading in our public schools.

"This is Your nation, and we will not turn it over to the hand of the evil one. Satan, you will obey the Word of the resurrected Lord. In the Name of Jesus Christ, the Son of the living God, we bind your power and your influence over this nation, and we command you to come forth...

come forth from the influence of the government,
come forth from the influence of the leaders,

come forth from the influence of the educators,
come forth from the influence of the scientists and
those who create.

"In the Name of Jesus, be bound, you foul principality
and power and spiritual wickedness, for we recognize that
we wrestle not against flesh and blood, but we wrestle
against principalities and powers, and spiritual
wickedness which is in the high places of the earth.

"And now, Father we stand upon Your great promise
to us that whatsoever we bind on earth shall be bound
in heaven and whatsoever we loose on earth shall be
loosed in heaven.

"Right now, in the Name of Jesus...

"We bind the spirit of rebellion that has gripped our
young people and we loose upon them the spirit of love
and humility and submission!

"We bind the spirit of contention and fighting which
has invaded our homes and we loose upon them the spirit
of love and unity and forgiveness and understanding!

"We bind the spirits of fear and torment that have
invaded the hearts and minds of Your people and we
loose upon them the spirits of faith and peace and love.

"We bind the blind spirit of egotism and self service
which has gripped our national leaders and we loose
upon them the spirit of humility and service which our
founding Fathers knew.

"We bind the spirit of promiscuousness and lewdness
which has swept over this nation bringing its tide of
pornography and sex sins, and we loose upon those
involved, the spirits of shame and repentance for their
acts. We bind the lewd thoughts which have invaded
minds today and loose upon them the spirit of purity that
they begin to think on those things that are pure.

"Father, in the Name of Jesus, upon this country
we loose the spirit of healing and health. We
loose the revival of Your anointing on hearts and lives.
We loose a new stirring in the heart of Your Church, a
new victory in their thinking, a new liberty in their walk

of faith as we agree together for a new tide of Your Holy
Spirit to sweep our land.

"In the Name of Jesus.

Amen."

Chapter 3

REVELATION IS EXCITING

Revelation is exciting. It is something new and fresh. God speaks to the heart of man and brings forth a new message to the world.

Revelation among Christians falls into two categories:

One: The Holy Spirit brings revelation to the Church through the operation of the spiritual gifts of prophecy, tongues and interpretation, the discerning of spirits, the word of wisdom, or the word of knowledge. The Apostle Paul speaks of these gifts of the Holy Spirit and their operation in the Church in *I Corinthians, Chapters 12-14.*

Two: The Holy Spirit gives revelation to an individual, one of God's prophets, a revelation that is destined to revolutionize the spiritual life of the entire world.

In every period of history when a certain revelation of God to the Church has died, God has raised up a man to resurrect that message—to rekindle the Church with the flaming fires of His love, and the demonstration of the supernatural power of God.

PROPHETS OF TODAY

The Bible says, *"Surely the Lord GOD will do nothing, but he revealeth his secret unto his servants the prophets." (Amos 3:7)*

If you study the messages which God gave to the Old Testament prophets, you will find that these revelations were not always comforting; many times they were quite discomforting. These revelations of God's judgment and wrath cut deep into the hearts of the people.

The people tried to silence that voice, the voice of the prophet whom God raised up to save them; but because Almighty God had spoken, it came to pass and the people simply could not stop the message of God.

Jeremiah attacked the morally and spiritually corrupt institutions of his day with, *"Thus saith the Lord."* For his effort, he was thrown into a dungeon, but that did not alter the fulfillment of his word to Israel that said they would go into captivity for seventy years. His word of revelation and prophecy was fulfilled to the very letter. God always has the last word.

These revelations have continued down through the centuries! One such revelation came from God to an Augustinian friar named Martin Luther. The specific revelation, *"The just shall live by faith,"* (Romans 1:17) had died! God wanted Martin Luther to stand up and declare with a mighty voice (the voice of God Himself) that the Church had become lifeless—God does not require works of legalism, traditionalism, ritual, and formality to justify His children. All God requires is faith in Jesus Christ...the works will follow, as fruit of the Holy Spirit in the life of every believer.

CLEANSING THE TEMPLE/PURIFYING
THE CHURCH

Jesus went into the Temple in Jerusalem on a Holy Day and found the moneychangers there exploiting their own people by charging excessive interest (finance charge) on currency exchange, in order that people from outlying districts might be able to buy animals to offer as sacrifices to God. They were doing business right there in the Temple of God. Jesus said, *"Is it not written, My house shall be called of all nations the house of prayer? but ye have made it a den of thieves." (Mark 11:17)*

He girded up His loins, overturned the moneychangers' tables, and the tables of them that sold animals, and drove them out of the Temple.

I wonder what Christ would do today if He should walk down the aisles during one of the Sunday morning worship services in many of our denominational churches and find the spiritual conditions that are present in our churches?

"The smoke of Satan has entered through a fissure in the church," said Pope Paul VI.

But when Jesus cleansed the Temple of the moneychangers, the Bible tells us in *Matthew 21:14*, the sick, maimed, the halt and the blind were commanded to be brought to Him there, and in the Temple Jesus healed them all. The Church of Jesus Christ—not a man, not a gift—is the healing center of Christ.

"For where two or three are gathered together in my name, there am I in the midst of them." (Matthew 18:20)

It is when we begin to shake ourselves loose of some of our denominationalism, and to wash our hearts before God with the pure water of His Word, to cast out the idolatry and spiritual blindness that has filled our hearts for many years, that the Spirit of Christ is free to move with liberty—delivering, healing, and saving the multitude through us.

THE REAL HEALING CENTER

I believe with all my heart, as one who has conducted deliverance services around the world, that the Church of Jesus Christ—not myself, not a special gift, not a specific anointing of a man—but the Church, is the healing center of our Lord in the world today.

God's intention is that every time the doors of the church are opened, with two or more **believers** gathered in His Name, that the power of the Holy Spirit will be present to heal, save, and deliver.

DOES GOD STILL SPEAK TO PEOPLE TODAY?

Do you believe God speaks to people today, just as He did in times past?

There have been several occasions in my life when God spoke to me in a clear, distinct, audible voice, just as though He was sitting right in front of me in my room, talking with me as when two ordinary people have a conversation. I refer to these times of revelation with special emphasis because everything in this ministry . . . past, present, and future . . . is a direct result of these meetings which I have had with the Shekinah Presence of God.

One particular experience when God spoke to me like this was in 1964 on an island in the West Indies called Grenada. I was in my hotel room praying before going to the crusade service.

God said, "Son, I want you to begin to make plans to go back to North America to conduct crusades."

This new commission has been one of the biggest hurdles this ministry has had to overcome. It was not that we do not love the people of North America, but at that time the major thrust of this ministry was to reach the multitudes in foreign countries who had never heard the Gospel. God has blessed this ministry with as great results in foreign crusades as any ministry in the history of the Church.

Would you leave this type of ministry where you had been preaching to tens and even hundreds of thousands of people night after night, seeing as many as fifty thousand souls give their hearts to Christ in a single service, to come back to the United States of America where there are so many churches, almost as many as gas stations?

When I heard God tell me that I was going to come back to America, I said, "God, not Morris Cerullo!" But then, when He didn't answer, I bargained with Him. I said, "Give me at least one reason why I should come back to North America." You see, I, like most preachers from the United States, thought the time of revival for North America was past—because it appeared that North America was Gospel-hardened.

A PROPHETIC WORD

God said to me, "Son, judgment is coming to North America." This was in 1964, years before the assassinations, riots, hijackings, kidnapings, young people's revolts, drug cultures, political Watergates and the breaking down of the structure of our society.

Judgment has come upon every area of our society in these recent years, and it continues in this very hour.

God also told me, "Son, I am going to send upon North America a New Anointing of My divine healing power."

From the time God spoke to me in Grenada in 1964, I have preached this message across North America: "A New Anointing is coming, a New Anointing is coming, a New Anointing is coming."

The prayer that has been upon my heart and upon my lips has been, "God, send the New Anointing!"

WE BEGAN TO SEE

In June, 1971, we began to see a New Anointing of God's healing power begin to break through with great magnitude and power right here in the United States of America. Not in the foreign countries, but right here in the United States where the civic auditoriums have become too small to hold the great crowds of people pressing in to hear the message to see God's power demonstrated and to receive miracles in their body, soul, mind and spirit.

Much more important than the size of the crowds is the way the Holy Spirit ministers to the needs of the people in the services. The response to the altar call for each service has been tremendous. Hundreds are literally running to the platform to declare that God (not a man, not a ministry, but God) is healing them of virtually every variety of sickness, disease, and ailment known to man. This New Anointing is flowing like a mighty stream in the North American crusades.

In the last chapters of this book you will read some of the thrilling testimonies of physical healings which have actually taken place in these meetings as *"the power of the Lord was present to heal them." (Luke 5;17)*

Other people testified that they have been set free from mental and spiritual oppressions of evil spirits that had tormented them for as long as twenty years.

IN THE SPIRIT WORLD OF NORTH AMERICA

Something is happening "in the spirit world" of North America; there is no natural explanation for it. A New Anointing of the divine healing power of God has been sent down from heaven to save men and women and to heal their bodies. *"The glory of this latter house shall be greater than of the former." (Haggai 2:9)* As Jesus Himself said, *"He that believeth on me, the works that I do shall he do also; and greater works than these shall he do; because I go unto my Father." (John 14:12)*

THESE ARE TIMES OF GREATER GLORY

We are living in the times of greater glory, in the times of the latter house, the latter Church before Jesus comes; we are living in the times of refreshing which God promised would come from the Presence of the Lord. God is pouring out the love of His heart upon His Church and upon the world before He returns. He will rapture a Bride filled with His fullness.

WHO IS THIS REVELATION FOR?

Now the question is, "If God has sent a revelation, who is it for?" Is it intended to be only for a select few superspirituals or leaders who are destined to carry the spiritual load for the rest of the Body of Christ?

No! I believe this revelation is for every true born-again believer in Jesus Christ. I believe we are seeing the preparation, the purification of the Bride of Christ. I know that the Church will be raptured in a greater demonstration of the power of Christ than that in which it was born.

Yes, the revelation and the power of the New Anointing is for you.

Chapter 4

A VISION OF THE RAPTURE

I have much to thank God for in my personal life and the worldwide evangelistic ministry that God has privileged us to participate in. I am particularly thankful for the guidance of the Holy Spirit and for those times of great decision when God has spoken to me.

As a result, we are in the middle of the stream of the move of God on the earth.

GOD'S VOICE SPEAKS TO ME

I feel the guidance and counsel of the Holy Spirit each day, and I hear the voice of God speak to my innermost being. When I say, however, that I have heard the audible voice of God, this is something very special.

The first time I actually heard God speak to me was when I came out of the Jewish Orthodox orphanage. God, through a vision and His voice, gave me the pattern and plan for my life.

Another time I heard God speak to me was when this call of God came to me to come back to North America.

God knew this would be one of the most difficult decisions that I would ever have to make, and it was the most difficult commandment that He had ever given to me. He said, "Son, I am going to send you back to North America with a New Anointing of My divine healing power."

In between these two special occasions, God also spoke and told me of the change in spiritual patterns and movements that were going to take place all around the world. Let me share one of these prophecies with you.

CHARISMATIC REVIVAL IS COMING!

I was in the city of Lima, Ohio, in 1957, conducting a crusade. I was staying in a little room in the YMCA. Early one morning I was awakened, and the shades were drawn and the dawn had not arrived. All of sudden the room was filled with a supernatural light...I fell on my face. A vision began to appear. Before me there was a multitude impossible to number. It was a large place and it seemed as if I could see the actual curvature of the earth.

They were standing under a cloud-filled sky. As I looked up to those clouds, I had the expectation that something would appear, and I thought that maybe this was a vision of the Rapture of the Church.

As I gazed at those clouds, raindrops began to descend. It was not like natural rain—for the giant drops were coming down with great deliberateness. As they reached the people, they became more like an oil that just seemed to flow over the multitude rather than the splashing of rain.

I cried out to God..."Lord, what does this rain mean?" A voice spoke to me out of the light, "This rain is the outpouring of My Holy Spirit."

Then I realized what I was seeing was the outpouring of the Holy Spirit upon the multitude. My first thought when I realized what this was, was to try and determine which denomination these people were (certainly I must find out so that I can join myself to that group, I thought). But try as I might, the longer I looked the more I realized that there was no denominational distinction—some were obviously Catholics, others Episcopalians, while others appeared to be from the fundamental denominations.

THE INSTRUMENT OF RIGHTEOUSNESS

The question on my heart was, "Lord, You have always in the past brought Your revelation to man through the vehicle of a particular group, but now there is no group."

There was no answer.

I said to myself—"If I cannot see the group, then surely I will see the man, the instrument that God has chosen to lead this new outpouring of the Holy Spirit."

I thought of the prominent men I knew whom God was using in that hour, and my eyes searched and searched that multitude to find one of them, but I could not distinguish them in the multitude.

Then I asked the Lord, "Are you trying to show me that You are choosing me to lead this new revival of Your Spirit?"

Then I heard the voice of God in that tiny room. If you tried to tell what direction it came from, it would be impossible for it just seemed to fill the whole room.

God said, "Son, you don't see the group or the man because there will not be anyone leading this revival. What I am about to do on the earth will be entirely without human direction, so that no man can take credit for it, no man or group can put their name on it. This will not be the work of a man, but of the Holy Spirit."

For moments that seemed like eternities, God told me many other things that were coming to pass, both in this revival of the Holy Spirit and in the fulfillment of prophecy. I relate only this part for it is sufficient to show how God allows His servant to see what is coming to pass in the spiritual realms, and not only to see what is coming to pass, but to see the eternal purposes of God in it.

THIS IS GOD'S GREATEST HOUR

I would rather be alive today than at any other period of history. Some would choose to have been with Jesus as He ministered in Jerusalem on the Mount of Olives or on the shores of Galilee. Another would say, "I would choose to have been there on the day of Pentecost when the Holy Spirit first came upon the disciples."

I would choose this hour because I believe we are in the midst of the beginnings of the greatest demonstration of the outpouring of God's miracle power the world has ever seen. Yes, I know about the miracles when God led the children of Israel out of Egypt; yes, I know the miracle of the fire on the altar as Elijah challenged the false prophets of Baal; yes, I know that Jesus turned the water into wine, and that He raised Lazarus from the dead.

I am also well aware of the exploits of the disciples in the book of Acts, and the miracles that accompanied the Apostle Paul as he brought the message of the resurrection power of Jesus Christ to the Gentiles...I know, I know, I know, but I still say God is going to close out this generation upon the earth, before He returns for His Church, with a demonstration of the greatest miracle power yet! Our minds have not yet begun to comprehend what is going to come to pass right before our very eyes.

THE FINAL HOUR

Beyond a shadow of a doubt this is the period of final preparation. We are on the threshold of God's final acts!

From our vantage point, we can see through the great door the glories and the judgments God has ready to be unveiled before an unbelieving world.

I say unbelieving world, but the sad part is how many unbelieving there will be right in our churches.

WHO WILL BE RAPTURED?

A few years after my vision in Lima, Ohio, I was asked to speak at a special dinner meeting in the Los Angeles area. Whenever I minister, my custom is always to spend several hours in prayer and meditation before God in order to prepare. I prefer to come to the platform just about the time that I am about to speak.

At this particular meeting, however, I came a little early and now I know what the reason was. God had something very definite for me to hear. A well-known, respected businessman was speaking; I thought he was giving his testimony, as is usually the case.

All of a sudden I heard this man say, "Last night I had a vision from the Lord; it was about the Rapture of the Church. The most significant thing was to see that less than half of the so-called Church was going up in the Rapture."

I don't know if it hit the rest of the gathering the way it did me, but it literally shocked me. I was dumbfounded. At first I was ready to write off the statement as the product of an emotional Christian.

But when I considered the man, whose reputation was thought to be of utmost integrity, I had to give weight to his experience.

I would be hard-pressed to tell you what my sermon was about that night because all I could think of was this man's vision. I don't believe that I have ever had a more difficult time preaching. How can you get the anointing on a subject when you are not even thinking about it—

your mind is somewhere else!

I closed that message as quickly as I could; I may have appeared awfully rude to many of my good friends at that meeting, but all I could think of was getting back to my hotel room and seeking the face of God for some answers.

When I arrived in my room, I dropped immediately to my knees and asked God some very troubling questions: "Lord, how could a responsible man and a Christian leader make such irresponsible statements?"

The Spirit of God spoke immediately to my heart and said, "Son, you do err not knowing the Scripture. Is it not written: *'Not every one that saith unto me, Lord, Lord, shall enter into the kingdom of heaven; but he that doeth the will of my Father which is in heaven?'* (Matthew 7:21) Is it not written: *'Unto them that look for him shall he appear the second time....'* " (Hebrews 9:28)

THE THIRD PART OF THE VISION

Now I understood the third part of the vision that God gave me in Lima, Ohio: The charismatic renewal is more than just the infilling of the Holy Spirit; **it is the separation of a people from the world that will be prepared to meet Christ.**

When I say separation, I do not mean going off to some desert retreat and living a monastic life. I mean a separation that is caused by your dedication to Christ and a moral standard of living.

As a result of this, Spirit-filled people are going to fall into two groups. One: There are going to be those who are not going to be willing to pay the price of separation from the things of the world. They are going to try to incorporate the best of two worlds, but they will find that it doesn't work. The power of God that has come into their lives will be dissipated. Two: Those who will refuse to sit on the fence, or compromise, but will be determined to live their lives by the Holy Spirit Who is within them in complete yieldedness to the will of God.

The lines of demarcation will be clearly drawn.

THE DANGERS OF REVIVAL

Along with the blessing, there is an inherent danger in revival. When something becomes very popular, whether in the religious or the secular field, the proper perspective can be quickly lost, and the real meaning and objective missed.

As a student of revivals in Church history, I am compelled to ask myself and God this question, "What is there about this revival or move of the Spirit which is to come, that will make its ultimate destiny different from all those which preceded it?"

WHY WILL THIS LAST REVIVAL BE DIFFERENT?

What can give us the confidence that this refreshing from above will not go the way of all of its predecessors?

Tell me of a visitation of the Lord that men did not try to organize, guide, refine, define, confine, use, abuse, and confuse until there was little left of what God originally intended it to be.

Men have always placed a label on it, tried to copyright it so that they could say, "Now, if you want this blessing you have to follow our rules and you have to come and go where we tell you to."

What makes us think that this revival will be any different?

ONLY ONE DIFFERENCE

There is only one factor that makes this present move of the Holy Spirit different: It is the last great move of the Holy Spirit upon mankind and its purpose is not simply to renew and to restore, but it is for the purpose of making ready a people prepared to meet the Lord.

That preparation has a twofold purpose. One: It will infuse the true Church of Jesus Christ with the power to do exploits for God. His miracle-working power shall be more prevalent among the true Church in this last hour than ever before in the history of the Church.

Two: It shall prepare the armor of the child of God to withstand the attacks of Satan which shall also be the strongest in all the ages. It shall be a revival of true holiness.

Prepare to put your armor on.

Chapter 5

A CALL TO ARMS

The true move of the Holy Spirit is a call to greater dedication and holiness in our Christian lives. Paul told Timothy, *"All that will live godly in Christ Jesus shall suffer persecution." (II Timothy 3:12)* If that was true in Paul's day, it will be much more true in the days which will precede the coming of the Lord.

I am not saying that the Church is going to go through the Great Tribulation, but I do believe that the Church is going to go through a refining process where it is cleansed and purified, a Bride without spot or wrinkle.

THE EXPERIENCE OF YOUR ENEMY

As we approach this intensified warfare with the enemy, we must remember that all things are not equal. You in your own strength, depending on a Sunday morning shot in your spiritual arm, are absolutely no match for Satan and his devices! Think of it, he has at least six thousand years and more experience than you in utilizing every trick that is available to destroy God's handiwork in the

35

natural or spiritual world.

Never forget that for one moment, alone, you are no match for him....

YOU CANNOT AFFORD TO BE OVERCONFIDENT

Before the October 1973 war, Israel was confident that nothing could penetrate her security, and bring death and destruction to her people.

A few days before the October war the ruling Labor party ran large election advertisements in the newspaper declaring, "There is peace on the Suez, our borders are secure, there is prosperity in our land...."

"For when they shall say, Peace and safety; then sudden destruction cometh upon them...." (I Thessalonians 5:3)

In the fateful hours before the war began, the story is told that as the leaders reviewed the intelligence reports telling of the coming attack, they said among themselves, "It just won't happen, it can't happen, and if it does the enemy will be crushed just like in the Six-Day War."

The tragic element that was overlooked was the enemy was no longer fighting with the same weapons used in 1967.

As the highly superior Israeli pilots swept in for the initial kill, they were picked-off like a flight of geese. The enemy knew their skill and knew that they could not meet them on an equal basis. They met them instead with newly-developed Russian missiles that could not be disarmed and destroyed like those in the past.

The School of Experience has a very high tuition. For Israel, it was the lives of twenty-five hundred of their best fighting men, officers and pilots.

For months after the war, the nation was torn asunder over placing the blame on someone's shoulders for the disaster. They won the war, but it still was a disaster that will be written in the pages of Israeli history. What took place was similar to the confident warriors of Joshua when they approached the city of Ai. It was to be a pushover, but instead they found themselves defeated. A period of soul-searching followed. There was sin in the camp.

The historians of the Six-Day War relate how an open Bible was found on the desks of the leading generals as they left their offices for the battlefields on June 5, 1967. All of the facts have not been evaluated concerning the war of 1973, but all indications are that Israel did not feel they needed any divine help to keep their enemies out of Israeli territory.

Miscalculating the enemy's power in either the natural or the spiritual world can mean disaster. In the natural world it can mean physical death, but in the spiritual world it results in eternal death.

A COMPROMISE IS A DEFEAT

The strategic mistake which many Christians make is that they are willing to settle for a compromise with the devil. To them a compromise is a victory. There is no such thing as a stalemate with the enemy of men's souls. There is no negotiable truce line of the Spirit when you have a compromise agreement, and you say to the devil, "You stay over there, and I'll stay over here."

You either win or you lose; to compromise is to lose; to accommodate is to lose. We are only winners if we have overcome the forces that are trying to defeat us.

Stop for a moment. Consider your present standards of Christian conduct. Line them up against what you stood for and believed ten years ago, or even five years ago, or just one year ago—does the comparison show a drastic difference?

Does this comparison indicate compromise, retreat, accommodation, surrender, adjustment, a lowering of standards by the pressure of your peers, or do you take the more sophisticated and intelligent viewpoint and say that this is simply staying current with the trends, staying up with the times, that standards are different now?

This is the heart of our subject. Are you going to be satisfied with a continual course of adjusting to the times and trends of this world, or do you want the power of God in your life for total victory? Are you feeling the urgent call of the Holy Spirit to begin to invade the territory of the enemy and redeem back those blessings that he has robbed from you, your family, friends, loved ones, your town, city, community, or country?

God has confirmed over and over again that the revelation of the New Anointing is for the purpose of unleashing the inherent power that God has sent to us in the renewal of the Holy Spirit that is sweeping the world.

EXPERIENCE IS DEPTH

In the School of Ministry, which we conduct in conjunction with our crusades in North America, the people can come and enjoy the fellowship of other believers and the ministry of the Spirit, but they are always surrounded with the other facts of life. The overflowing joy which they receive as they sit at the feet of the Holy Spirit has an immediate power to reach the unsaved the minute they leave the meeting. They come into contact with people in the city and in a very practical, simple Christian manner with the love of God—they can allow that river of living water to begin to flow to meet human need, and share Jesus Christ with others.

In the evening they are taken into the large arena where thousands of people from all over the metropolitan area of that city have gathered. In that meeting they see the keys which they have been taught about in the morning, put into use, they see the strong bondage of the devil in sickness, disease, habits, and sin begin to crumble under the explosive impact of the Presence of the Holy Spirit of the living God.

They get the theory, the biblical foundation of the teaching in the morning and the demonstration of the power of God in the evening. In the evening services the Holy Spirit bears witness to the truth of the teaching of the New Anointing. This is also immediately applicable to every problem, burden, and need of their lives!

If you have already received an experience of the Holy Spirit, which has been called the Baptism of the Holy Spirit, consider very carefully the fact that what you have received is only the beginning of what God has in store for you. That initial blessing is only Step Number One. You have entered the "boot camp" of the Spirit. You are in the training period, a time of preparation for what God really wants to do through you.

KEYS IN ACTION

As you continue to read on in this book, you are going to find it very difficult not to put into practice the keys of spiritual victory that will be given to you.

God has sent this book your way for a very definite purpose.

START NOW

Mother, you can begin doing something constructive about that son of yours who is in rebellion and that daughter who has run away from home and you don't know where she is. Yes, I know that you have prayed and prayed, but now God wants you to enter into spiritual warfare for their salvation, and I know that you will see the victory.

FAMILIES

This message is for that young wife who thought that everything in her marriage was just beautiful and as happy as could be. It was until about six months ago when all of a sudden something seemed to change. At first it was difficult to put a finger on the problem, but it all seemed to fall into place when the husband came home from work and announced that he was asking for a divorce and that he was in love with another woman.

Recognize this clearly for what it is: a work of the enemy. I have good news for you. You are neither helpless nor alone. Jesus said, *"I will never leave you, nor forsake you. I will not leave you comfortless...."*

Since God began to pour this message of the New Anointing into my heart, I have seen homes come together the very night we prayed. Up until that time neither partner had the slightest hope of ever seeing a reconciliation.

A CALL TO ARMS

The Holy Spirit is sending out a call to spiritual arms throughout the world, and God wants to use **you!**

Jesus said in the book of Revelation, *"Behold I stand at the door and knock: if any man hear my voice, and open the door, I will come in to him, and will sup with him, and he with me." (Revelation 3:20)*

Often we will use this verse in speaking to the sinner, but in reality this verse is referring to the believer. Through the infilling of the Holy Spirit, Christ comes into communion in the life of the believer. The door has to be opened to let Christ in. Now that He is in us, we must allow the power of Christ to become active in our lives. Even as it was possible for us as unbelievers to keep Him on the outside, so now it is possible for us to keep that power shackled in our lives so that the rivers of living water, the power of God, will not flow out for the deliverance of our personal needs and those of our loved ones.

The New Anointing is here.

Who needs it?

We all do...

today, tomorrow, and every day until Jesus comes.

Chapter 6

ENTERING THE FLOW OF GOD'S POWER

Early in the book of Acts, we find the disciples of Jesus huddled in an upper room.

Behind locked doors for fear of the Jewish leaders and Roman soldiers who had so recently torn their beloved leader from them, they no doubt were the picture of discouragement and despair.

Many of them were tired from their long journey to Jerusalem or from the sleepless nights of terror which preceded this particular gathering. There was perhaps a great sense of defeat that the enemy had smitten the shepherd and scattered the sheep. They were completely disorganized, for the One to Whom they had looked for leadership was gone.

They also must have been bitterly disappointed at the size of the gathering.

Jesus had told more than 500 to wait for the promise of the Father. Yet, only 120 of the most stalwart were endeavoring to carry out that last command from those beloved lips.

They were discouraged too...for those same lips had told them to go out and evangelize the world...a gargantuan task which they felt helpless to carry out. What a picture of despair and defeat!

Yet, ten days later we see these same disciples no longer hovering behind closed doors but noisily spilling down into the street with such joy that travelers from throughout that area of the world looked on in utter astonishment.

Peter, who just days before had denied vehemently any connection with Jesus, stood forth and boldly proclaimed that although Jesus had been crucified, God had raised Him from the dead and even now He was exalted by the right hand of God.

So full of persuasion were this man's words, so full of joy his companions, that as he preached, about three thousand souls were added to the Church that day.

This tremendous change was not a momentary thing, for we read on in the book of Acts that this revival continued and *"the Lord added to the church daily such as should be saved." (Acts 2:47)*

We read that Peter and John confronted a man, lame since birth, who was begging outside the Temple, and in the Name of Jesus commanded the man to walk. *"Then Peter said, Silver and gold have I none; but such as I have give I thee: In the name of Jesus Christ of Nazareth rise up and walk. And he took him by the right hand, and lifted him up: and immediately his feet and ankle bones received strength. And he leaping up stood, and walked, and entered with them into the temple, walking, and leaping, and praising God." (Acts 3:6-8)*

Still later we read of Peter that *"Insomuch that they brought forth the sick into the streets, and laid them on beds and couches, that at the least the shadow of Peter passing by might overshadow some of them." (Acts 5:15)*

A REED NO LONGER SHAKEN

Could this be that same Simon Barjona whose very name had meant "a reed" and who had exhibited the characteristics of a reed in his wavering testimony to Christ? Could this be he who had grabbed his sword and impulsively smitten off the ear of Malchus the night Jesus was arrested?

Could this be the same Simon who, after Jesus was crucified, announced, *"I go a-fishing" (John 21:3)* and had returned to the occupation he held before the glorious call to follow Jesus had come to him?

Could it be the same man?

It was...and it wasn't.

This was indeed the same outward vessel, but some tremendous, earth-shaking transformation had taken place in this man's being.

A RADICAL DIFFERENCE

He had the same facial features; he wore the same clothing; he had the same fisherman's background...but something was radically different.

What had happened?

We can read about it in *Acts 2:1-4: "And when the day of Pentecost was fully come, they were all with one accord in one place. And suddenly there came a sound from heaven as of a rushing mighty wind, and it filled all the house where they were sitting. And there appeared unto them cloven tongues like as of fire, and it sat upon each of them. And they were all filled with the Holy Ghost, and began to speak with other tongues, as the Spirit gave them utterance."*

Peter, and the other 119 disciples who were obedient to Jesus' command to tarry until they were endued with power from on high *(Luke 24:49)*, had received a personal, vibrant, life-changing encounter with the third Person of the Godhead, the Holy Spirit of God.

We call this experience today the Baptism with the Holy Spirit, a phrase that strikes different responses in different hearts.

To some Pentecostals it brings a sense of self-satisfaction: "That's us! We've got it! We've had this thing fenced for years. It's ours."

To members of many mainline churches, it brings a note of fear: "Emotionalism"; "Not for today"; False doctrine"; "Excesses"; "Fanaticism"; "Too much religion can drive you crazy"; "Social ostracism."

What the phrase should mean to us is that here is a precious revealed truth of God, a promised gift, meant neither to frighten us nor to make us smug, but to lift us from the planes of our own resources and implant within us the very power of God here on earth.

The disciples who tarried in the upper room had entered into the very life stream of God's power here on earth, a stream that has never been shut off since and which is available today to every born-again believer.

Each one can, and should be, baptized...immersed... overwhelmed...consumed into that stream of power which Jesus has opened for us that we might live vibrant, persuasive lives for Him and that we might touch the lives of others with His transforming power.

OBSTACLES TO OVERCOME

Without a doubt, one of the greatest obstacles to people really entering into the power that God has for them is the fear that they will become too emotional, like some they have heard or seen.

Man is prone to excesses and some forms of worship, when there is not the sweet flow of the Spirit, bring more attention to the flesh than glory to God.

On the other end of the spectrum is one who is so

bound by fear that he can never really enter in and embrace the beauty of true worship of the Lord.

A minister friend once said that he would rather attempt to control fire than to try to raise the dead, and I think he has a point there.

One of the great joys that I have experienced frequently in recent years is to see what happens to a Christian when he comes out of a bondage and really begins to worship God in spirit and in truth.

Mrs. W. Witherspoon of Dallas, Texas, expressed the transition as well as anyone. She wrote us a letter following the Dallas crusade and said, "Brother Cerullo, my husband and I are Methodists. About the closest thing to your crusade that we ever attended was a Billy Graham meeting in El Paso several years ago. We are very unemotional people. The first night, as you walked out onto the platform, I heard a mighty wind flow through that building and a wonderful Presence just filled the auditorium!"

Her husband was miraculously healed of back trouble during that crusade and no longer wears the back brace he had to wear for ten years, even while he slept.

THE WARMTH OF THE HOLY SPIRIT

Linda Thomas was at the end of herself when she came to our crusade in Tampa, Florida. Raised in an evangelical home, her marriage was filled with conflict, especially when it was time to decide what religion their first child was to be raised. Her husband was Catholic.

Linda felt the pressures coming from every direction, and alcohol became her constant source of relief. It was her friend until the dependence was established, and then it became her master.

As she stood in the audience of our crusade that night, she was on the edge of a nervous breakdown. For all practical purposes her marriage was gone, her family was destroyed, and she held little hope that religion could solve her problems.

Religion couldn't, but the power of the Holy Spirit could and did. All around her in that service people were getting healed. A flicker of hope ignited in her heart.

Could it be possible?

All of a sudden she felt the warmth of the Holy Spirit come all over. Nobody touched her, but from the platform a hundred feet away I could see the anointing of the Holy Spirit upon her. It was as though there was a light shining all around her.

We discovered later than Linda had been on pills and alcohol so long that she had developed a stomach infection with bleeding and constant pain. As she sat in the crusade service and saw with her own eyes that God is a real and vital force, able to perform miracles and change lives, she began to feel something within herself change. As the Holy Spirit moved, new faith began to well up in her heart, and she dedicated her life to Jesus. As she did so, a peace settled over her shattered nerves.

Not only was she healed of the pain and infection that night, but all desire for alcohol left her. Her husband also was saved during the crusade and shortly afterwards they renewed their marriage vows.

Linda later testified before that huge congregation how the Holy Spirit had lifted her from the depths of despair and so changed her heart and her circumstances that she was "walking on air."

WALKING AND LEAPING

Cletta Roberts was carried on a stretcher into our last service in the Denver, Colorado crusade. She did not believe in Holy Spirit healing, but what did she have to lose? Several back operations had only left her worse, and she was in contant pain. At the very end of the meeting, the Holy Spirit witnessed to my spirit that someone with a large steel back-brace was being healed. Within a few minutes' time, Cletta had gone into the ladies lounge to remove her brace and rushed to the platform where she was able to bend freely and painlessly. She had come on a cot, but she left literally walking and leaping and praising God!

Her reserved background was not showing then nor has it much since, because God perfectly healed her in that service.

Do not be afraid of going off the deep end. A leading Christian psychologist of many years experience said that he is yet to see the person who has too much of Christ in his or her life.

I promise you that if you get off that fence, and let go of your spiritual pride, If you enter into this revelation with your whole heart, the Holy Spirit will transform your life.

MORE ANSWERS TO PRAYER

Since this revelation of the New Anointing has come to pass, we have seen more answers to prayer in this ministry than ever before. My objective is not just to have God give you a blessing. God will bless you through this message, I am sure. But more importantly, I am concerned that you begin to have the power of God produced in your life in a greater measure than ever before. The Bible says, *"Ye shall receive power, after that the Holy Ghost is come upon you." (Acts 1:8)*

Most of God's people pray for the **power**, but stop short with the blessing...even when they experience the phenomenon of the gift of tongues as they are praying and seeking God for the Baptism of the Holy Spirit.

Jesus did not only say that ye shall receive the gift of tongues, but that you shall receive **power** as well.

Power, after that the Holy Ghost is come upon you!

During Old Testament times, God often visited the power of His Spirit upon a certain person for a certain work at a certain time. It was by the power of God that Moses called forth plagues that were visted on Egypt and later performed miracles to sustain the children of Israel in their desert wanderings. It was God's power that enabled Elijah to call down fire from heaven upon his sacrifice on Mt. Carmel and to open and close the heavens to rain. It was God's power that came upon Samson and enabled him to carry off the gates of Gaza and to slay 1000 Philistines with the jawbone of a donkey.

But this Spirit did not rest upon all His children. It was a special provision for special times.

When Jesus came, the Holy Spirit still was not given in power to all believers. Rather, the Spirit worked in Jesus and those whom He commissioned for specific spiritual tasks.

ANOTHER COMFORTER

Jesus told them, "When I go away, something else is going to happen, another Comforter is going to come." *"And I will pray the Father, and he shall give you another Comforter, that he may abide with you for ever." (John 14:16)*

"But the Comforter, which is the Holy Ghost, whom the Father will send in my name, he shall teach you all things, and bring all things to your remembrance, whatsoever I have said unto you." (John 14:26)

In *Luke 24:49*, He says, *"And, behold, I send the promise of my Father upon you: but tarry ye in the city of Jerusalem, until ye be endued with power from on high."*

And in *Acts 1:8*, His promise was *"But ye shall receive power, after that the Holy Ghost is come upon you: and ye shall be witnesses unto me both in Jerusalem, and in all Judaea, and in Samaria, and unto the uttermost part of the earth."*

It was at the Word of Jesus that the 120 had gathered in the upper room, not really knowing exactly what to expect nor exactly how to pray. They had no pattern to show them how to receive this promise, for it had not been given before. There was no one to try to massage the Holy Spirit into them and advise them, "Now say glory, glory, glory over and over until you lose control of your tongue." There was a just a band of believers who got in one spirit and one accord and meant business with God.

NOT THE 'GOOD OLD DAYS'

I cannot believe these disciples wasted any time sitting around and discussing the "good old days," the power they used to have when Jesus was here but which they felt they no longer possessed. They were too busy receiving the promise that God had for them at the moment, in their present and in their future, not the past. God has a "today" experience for us if we will enter into it. The fountain is wide open!

WHERE IS THE REAL POWER?

I used to wonder why even churches which believed and taught the Baptism of the Holy Spirit had no real power. Then I found the answer. We stopped at what we called "the blessing." After people received a few syllables of speaking in tongues, they thought they had it. Their dedications at the altar stopped, their all night prayer meetings stopped, waiting before God stopped, passionate reading of the Bible stopped, and all the consistent consecration to God seemed to ebb away more and more.

Why?

Because they felt that they did not need to spend the time in dedicated prayer and consistent consecration because they had spoken in tongues, had the Baptism, had arrived!

What they did not realize was that they needed the prayer and the waiting and the dedication now more than ever in order to properly channel, control and use the power of the Holy Spirit which God had placed within them!

Now I think you can begin to see why I am placing more emphasis on receiving power in our lives than I am in just receiving a blessing. The blessing will take care of itself, but we must begin now to allow the Holy Spirit to produce the power of God in our lives, day after day.

Only when you have passed beyond the realm of blessing into the realm of power will you be ready to invade the devil's territory and come away the victor.

SPIRITUAL VISION

The Baptism of the Holy Spirit is a totally spiritual experience. There is physical evidence...but that evidence is of a spiritual experience! Therefore this experience can never be fully comprehended by the natural mind or the reasoning of the senses.

It goes far beyond the physical evidence. It becomes a spiritual power.

That power is God Himself working in our lives, through our lives, to effect changes not only in us but in others with whom we come in contact. Every one of us as believers need to enter into this open flow of God's power and continue in it deeper and deeper and deeper.

Right now, before we go any further with this message, I have a special prayer for every person whom God leads to read this book on the revelation of the New Anointing. *"But the natural man receiveth not the things of the Spirit of God: for they are foolishness unto him: neither can he know them, because they are spiritually discerned." (I Corinthians 2:14)*

I pray that the light of the Holy Spirit will shine upon your eyes, that you may be able to see as you have never seen before. I pray that every blinding spiritual cataract will be removed from your eyes, in the Name of Jesus, Amen.

Chapter 7

THE CHARISMATIC REVIVAL AND YOU!

I believe, and have taught for many years, that the Church of Jesus Christ will be raptured in a greater demonstration of miracle power than it was born in!

In recent years, there have been tremendous break-throughs in the realm of space technology. We not only have put men in space, we have landed them on the moon and sent satellites soaring past Mars and beyond, adventures unheard of just a few short years ago.

We have seen tremendous breakthroughs in the field of medicine, development of so-called miracle drugs and such sophisticated techniques of surgery that even human organs are now transplanted almost routinely. Many other major breakthroughs have occured in other sciences and fields.

Just as there have been breakthroughs in the natural realm, so there are going to be great breakthroughs in the spiritual realm.

There will be breakthroughs in revelation before Jesus comes, breakthroughs in miracles, breakthroughs in holiness. We are going to see new breakthroughs in power,

healing and the love of God in the Church of Jesus Christ.
I believe this with all my heart.

THE BIBLE SECRET TO SPIRITUAL POWER

The Church has not begun to fully experience what
God has for us.

Man limits an unlimited God.

One of the basic reasons is because we do not see our
Heavenly Father as He really is.

The God we serve is a God who knows no limits.

NEGATIVE + POSITIVE = POWER AND LIGHT

I am not an electrician, but electricians tell me you
cannot produce light and you cannot produce electricity
unless you have the negative as well as the positive.

Once you put the negative and the positive together,
then you have the combination that gives us electricity
that produces light.

In the Church we have the negative factor.

No. 1: We have limited an unlimited God.

No. 2: We do not see God as He really is.

No. 3: Too long we have wrestled for the power and
we have come up with only the blessing.

Do we really want the Bible secret of spiritual power?

If God is going to give us real spiritual power, then we
are going to have to hear the truth. The Bible says, *"Ye
shall receive* **power,** *after that the Holy Ghost is come
upon you...." (Acts 1:8)*

Because of the lack of teaching, we have been like
Jacob. We have wrestled until the sweat poured down our
brows. We have wrestled until even the spiritual thighs
of our beings came literally out of joint, **but we stopped
short of the power because we were willing to settle
for just a blessing.**

ONE STEP BEYOND BLESSING

The one step beyond blessing is clearly outlined for us by the Apostle Paul in the following verse: *"That I may know him, and the power of his resurrection, and the fellowship of his sufferings, being made conformable unto his death." (Philippians 3:10)*

No man can have a greater desire or a greater ambition than what the Apostle Paul just gave us in this verse— *"That I may know him...."*

Remember, we are talking about the New Anointing of the power of the Holy Spirit. We are not talking about how to get a blessing.

The future success of the revival movements in North America will lie in the hands of those who find the answer to this question: "What must we do that we might work the works of God?"

We have had our silver-tongued preachers. We have had our great orators who could take the English language and swirl it around our heads until we walked out of the meeting drunk with their verbosity. All we could say was, "My, wasn't that great? Didn't it sound good? Another person would say, "Yes, but what did he say?" The third person would add, "I don't know, but it sure was great." And this happens while of the almost six billion people of the world, half of them have never heard the Name of Jesus.

A NEW DEMAND FOR LEADERSHIP

The world cries for leadership. The charismatic moving of the Holy Spirit demands now that we come up with more than just a little babbling. It demands that we come up with men and women who out of all of this have **power with God and power with men and can prevail!**

TRUE KNOWEDGE OF GOD

When I read this text of the Apostle Paul, it first puzzled me. He cries, *"That I may know him, and the power of His resurrection, and the fellowship of his sufferings, being made conformable unto his death."* *(Philippians 3:10)*

I said to myself, "Is the Apostle Paul just starting out on his journey?" The truth is that the Apostle Paul is coming to the end of his journey. He had lived almost his complete life when he wrote this. Does not Paul know the Lord? Is there a difference in knowing the Lord and what the Apostle Paul is truly crying out to God for? What is this quest? What is this longing?

What is this passion of his being that surely is not the result of a happenstance, hit or miss contact with Christ, or of an emotional meeting?

I will tell you what it is. When the Apostle Paul was crying out, *"That I might know Him,"* it was a revelation of Paul's innermost being. He was revealing that on the inside, above everything else, he longed for an experience with God that would take him into the depths of Christ Who had paid such a price to redeem him.

Could this be one of the first steps to the Bible secret of true spiritual power? First of all, there must be a cry that comes up from our innermost being, far deeper than that which touches just the emotions—a cry that comes so deep from our souls that we say, "God, above everything else and more than anything else, I want to know You in a way where my whole being is interwoven and completely enraptured with You, Jesus."

HEAD KNOWLEDGE AND HEART KNOWLEDGE

Have you ever seen a storm? You can stand on a seashore and watch a storm. As the winds begin to blow and the waves begin to roll, you declare, "There's a storm."

You have a certain understanding of that storm.

Now let's draw another picture. Another person is actually out in the middle of that sea in a boat. The winds begin to blow and the sea begins to billow and roll. When this person gets to shore, he can say, "That is a storm!"

Both you and the second party have a certain understanding of the storm, the individual on the shore and the person in the middle of the sea.

But there is a distinct difference between the two.

The one who stands on the shore and looks on has only **knowledge**.

The other person who is out in the midst of the storm and has had his life tossed back and forth by the waves and the wind came out with **experience**.

I pray, "Oh, God, it is not for head knowledge that we cry. It is not for the ability to understand only with our minds, but we long for the experience—that which actually takes our being and interweaves it with the Person of Jesus"

CUT AWAY YOUR SHORELINES

We have to be a little like Joshua. Joshua had to be willing to step out on faith. The power of God never did come and demonstrate itself for him as it did for Moses until he was willing to cut away from his shorelines.

What are your shorelines? Past traditions? Church orientation? Dogma? Denominationalism? Your preconceived ideas of God that put Him in a specific mold and say, "Unless God does it this way, I can't accept it." I don't believe God works like that!

What is the shoreline? '

It is only at this particular point that the Jordan River parts.

It is only at this particular point that the great big hand of God comes down from heaven and rolls back the river of obstacles, burdens, problems too big for you to handle and allows you to pass over into the Promised Land. It is only at this particular point when theory becomes reality—when you are willing to cut away your own personal shorelines.

"Oh, God, take the blinding spiritual cataracts from our eyes, melt them by the Holy Spirit that we may be able to see as we have never seen before and launch out. Let that water come up over our ankles, so that You can begin to give us experience and not just head knowledge—not just the blessing, but the power."

THE NEW WAY

There are three important basic principles to be learned in the leading and moving of the Holy Spirit in an individual's life.

One: God never does anything **to us**. Two: God never does anything **for us**. Three: He always works **in** and **through** us.

We are in a different dispensation. In the Old Testament days, in the time of Abraham, Isaac, and Jacob, God worked by coming upon the scene and anointing His prophets and priests.

God anointed Elijah for certain tasks and then the Holy Spirit Who came upon him left him. It never did abide with him continually.

It was the same for Samson. It was the same for the other great prophets and patriarchs of old.

Then in the New Testament era, the Holy Spirit did not come because Christ was with us. The Holy Spirit came upon Christ and demonstrated and acted through Him in our midst.

Jesus said, *"If I go away, the Comforter will not come unto you; but if I depart, I will send him unto you."* *(John 16:7)*

God never does anything **to** us.

    There is a reason.

        We will find out why.

God never does anything **for** us.

    There is a reason.

        We will find out why.

God always works **through** us.

The secret of seeing the demonstration of God's love, His power, or any part of His being comes in only one way—it comes as God demonstrates all these facts through us!

The Apostle Paul said, *"...according to His working, which worketh in me mightily." (Colossians 1:29)*

He said, *"We have this treasure in earthen vessels." (II Corinthians 4:7)*

It is God working through us. Too long we have struggled for the power.

How many people would like to be like Jesus? How many have connived and maneuvered and tried to be like Jesus? Every one of us including myself would have to say, "Yes, I have been guilty."

Our struggling to be like Him is not going to produce Him.

GOD'S LIFE, OR OUR STRUGGLE?

It is not struggling. I want to give you a statement of truth at this point that can revolutionize your life.

Man has nothing in himself but that he receives it from above.

It is not struggling, but it is God's life flowing through us.

One day Jesus came to a well. He sat there, and it wasn't long before a little woman came and Jesus began to talk to her. This woman was a Samaritan and Jesus asked her for a drink of water. The first thing this lady did was say to Jesus, "How come you, being a Presbyterian, ask me, a Pentecostal, for a drink of water?" She said, "Don't you know the Presbyterians and Pentecostals don't have anything to do with each other?"

Now in reality she did not say that exactly, but in essence she did. Doesn't that sound familiar?

Here's what she really said, *"How is it that thou, being a Jew, askest drink of me, which am a woman of Samaria?" (John 4:9)*

We have the idea that denominational differences are a product of the 20th, or the 16th, or 17th centuries. As the preacher said, "It just ain't so."

Jesus looked at this woman and said, *"If thou knewest the gift of God, and who it is that saith to thee, Give me to drink; thou wouldest have asked of him, and he would have given thee living water." (John 4:10)*

If we only knew—if we only could see Him. If we only understood. If the whole church world—Baptists, Methodists, Pentecostals, Assemblies of God, Four Square, Church of God, Open Bible, Presbyterians, Catholics, Lutherans, Pentecostal Holiness, all denominations— really understood Who we are supposed to be serving!

HOW ARE YOU GOING TO GET THE WATER OUT OF THE WELL?

The woman of Samaria was very inquisitive. She went around this side of the well and then walked around the other side of the well.

"How are you going to get water out of a well if you don't have a bucket?" she wanted to know.

I am not much of a farmer just like I am not much of an electrician. Farmers tell me there are two kinds of wells in the world. For one kind you need a bucket and a long rope. You let the bucket down into the well and you do what most preachers have to do—you pump it up: "Say 'Praise the Lord'...Say 'Hallelujah'...Say 'Amen'...Let's praise the Lord"...and on and on the pump is worked!

SUPERSTARS OR THE BODY OF CHRIST

Most people think that preachers are magicians.

Nowhere in the Scriptures do you find that God wants preachers to go out and be the superstars while the church world lies there and goes to sleep and does not participate. The early Church was a laymen's movement.

CONVERTS OR DISCIPLES

Jesus did not tell His disciples to go out and make converts. He told them to go out and make disciples. When we get someone saved, we should not be making just a convert.

To make a convert is to persuade or induce a person to adopt our particular faith or belief. To make a **disciple** is something entirely different. Here that person becomes a learner; he becomes a follower; he becomes a sharer! He is not just making mental assent to the fact that Jesus is the Savior, but he is so stirred by the revelation of Jesus that he wants to sit at the feet of Jesus in worship and adoration, learning of what his Master has instructed him to do!

Does the Bible tells us that when we come into His courts that we should wait for the preacher—wait for the evangelist—wait for the superstar to come out and start flowing to prime us and pump us?

Many church members sit up Saturday night watching the Late Late Show and walk into church Sunday morning with bloodshot eyes. They drag in late, sit down, and cannot participate in worship. **They are spectators**.

No, sir! The Bible does not tell us this is the way it should be.

The Bible says that when you enter into God's courts,

enter in with praise and with thanksgiving upon your hearts. When you come, bring a psalm. When you come, bring a testimony. When you come, bring a word from the Lord. Another one brings a free spirit. When you all come together you flow in your worship, and then you have spiritual spontaneous combustion that results in the moving of the Holy Spirit.

Farmers tell me there is another kind of well. You do not need a bucket for this well. It's an artesian well. You do not need a rope, and you do not need a bucket. You have to have a lid on top of it to hold it down because it is shooting up and springing up of its own accord. You do not pump it; it is already primed. It shoots up by its own accord!

You become a participator—not a spectator.

WHERE STRUGGLES CEASE

Jesus looked at that woman walking around the well and said, "Don't look for the bucket. The water I give you shall be in you a well of Living Water springing forth unto everlasting life."

No more struggling to be like Him. No more asking God for the transformation of human flesh.

"This water that I shall give you shall be in you a well of living water that is permeating your whole being— springing forth unto everlasting life."

WHAT IS THE SOURCE OF THIS POWER?

Everything about man is corrupt, so the power does not come from man.

What then is the source of the river? The flow is in God.

It is His river. It is not man's to control and use as he wishes.

It is His divine life. It is not man. It is His river of divine healing. We have become spectators; we have stood by and watched God use the great evangelist while we have sat back complacently and watched.

Our eyes become so focused on the manifestation of a certain man's gift that we fail to see that the river of divine healing is God's river.

It is His river of salvation.

It is His river of power.

It is His river of glory.

"The earth is the LORD'S, and the fulness thereof." *(Psalm 24:1)* **It is all His!**

HERE IS THE SECRET

Do not try to take the water out of the river.

That is what we have done for so long. We have taken the water out of the river. This is why we have been faced with so much failure. We have come up with the blessing and have not had the power to say to the demon possessed person "Come out" and watch that person be set free.

You cannot take the water out of the river. Once you do, it ceases to be a river, and it is nothing more than a stagnant product of man. I, for one, am tired of watching the manipulation of man. I am hungry for the true manifestations of the Holy Spirit that are expressed in and through the Body of Christ.

TAPPING THE SOURCE

We must abide in Him and let His Words abide in us. Then we begin to tap the source. Then we shall ask what we will and it shall be done unto us.

Do you want to go into the depths of God like the Apostle Paul—"Lord, that I may know him—that I may know him..." Do you truly want this?

As the body is more than meat and raiment, so the real man is more than the body.

I want you to look at your physical body. Just look at your hands. Did you ever stop to think as you look at that body that you are actually not that body?

We are not our bodies. The body is a habitation in which the real you dwells. Let me illustrate.

I hold in my hand a beautiful watch. I am proud of it, but it is just a very simple watch. I wear it wherever I go. It has special meaning to me. It was given to me by one of my dearest minister friends in Canada. But do you know something? When you look at this watch you have not seen the watch at all.

You say, "Brother Cerullo, I can see it—it looks like a watch!"

In order for you to really see the watch, I would have to take the back off and let you look inside. Once you saw the inside and all the intricate mechanisms that go into this timepiece to make it indicate the time, then you could really say, "I have seen the watch."

The watch is not the crystal. The watch is not the face. The watch is not the hands. The watch is the intricate mechanism on the inside.

It is the intricate spiritual mechanism in the very depths of your being that we are talking about right now. We believe in outward expression. We believe in the blessing, but all that is external becomes valid only when it is springing forth from the well that is filled with the water of life—the eternal source of power that has formed the universe.

ONE STEP MORE

Go beyond the blessings and attain the power that will

make you the person that God wants you to be in this last hour.

In our crusade services we continually tell the audiences that **God is a Spirit** and that He is everywhere present. His power can be received in the last row of the third balcony just as it is in the first row on the main floor or right beside me on the platform.

The same is true as you read this book. Whether you are near or far away, if you feel your well has run dry, the Spirit of God is right there to meet your present need and to place your feet on solid ground. You will bring blessing and deliverance to everyone that comes in contact in anyway with your life.

GOD IS SPIRIT

Our Father God, we thank You that You are a Spirit as You told that Samaritan woman who met You at the well. I know that there is no distance in the Spirit, and that You can touch our friends reading this book, whether they be near to us or far away; touch them I pray, through the Spirit of God with the New Anointing. In Jesus' Name. Amen.

Now get ready for the missing link.

Chapter 8

THE MISSING LINK

At this point in time the world stands at its most serious crossroads. Social, economic, and political changes are taking place so fast that the highest level of intelligence data gathered one day is out of date by the time it reaches the desk of a national leader the following day.

From the beginning of what we call "modern missions," the Church has had a two-dimensional approach to evangelism. There was one form of soul-winning at home in the local church, but an entirely different approach was made to foreign missionary work. The two always seemed irreconcilable.

As a boy, coming out of a Jewish Orthodox orphanage into the stream of organized evangelical Christianity, this divergence was clear. But it was such an established thing, I just accepted it.

I cannot say the ministry God led me into on the foreign fields was in the regular way of doing things, it took on a different approach than the way I ministered in America.

When God spoke to me on the Island of Grenada in the West Indies in 1964, He said,

"Son, I want you to get ready to go back to North America.

"I am going to send a New Anointing of My divine healing power to North America."

WHAT IS THE KEY TO REVIVAL?

I knew beyond the shadow of a doubt that God had spoken, but I also knew there was more the Spirit of God would reveal to His servant, for there was a missing link.

In the foreign mass evangelism meetings God had given us certain keys to reach a nation for Christ. I knew that if God was going to send this same anointing into American meetings, there would have to be a key again to reach this nation for Christ.

For the next eight years I was to search for that key.

God revealed the answer to me in the strangest place and under the most unusual conditions.

I was scheduled to conduct a crusade in India—one that I looked forward to with the greatest apprehension. I knew that every crusade of this nature that had ever been attempted in India by a foreigner like myself had been practically a defeat. I didn't know of one that had been completely successful.

The meetings were to be held on the South India Athletic Grounds—an open area about the size of at least three football fields put together.

AN OPEN CONFESSION

The Bible says confession is good for the soul. I don't mind telling you I was a little afraid, yet I was willing to obey God even if it meant the possibility of the Hindus or the Moslems rising up against me and tearing the platform down as they had done many times before to other missionary evangelists.

Even if it meant my life I was willing to give it, but thank God, He gave us the victory in India. We did not have one problem in the entire crusade, and God filled the area as large as three football fields with people standing shoulder to shoulder to hear the Gospel of Jesus Christ...without one problem!

SOMETHING IN THE AIR

My oldest son, David, went to India with our technician to do the set-up work for the crusade. David had just graduated from high school and was getting ready to go to a university. He met me at the airport when I arrived and I will never forget the look on his face. When I first saw him, I thought I was seeing a ghost. I asked him, "David, what's wrong?"

He said, "Dad, I don't know. There is something in the air—something in the atmosphere of this nation. I have been with you in South America, in Europe, and in other places, but there is something here that makes me sick. I do not understand it."

I knew what he felt. I had been in India before. I knew of the 330 million false gods that are worshiped by the Indian people. The oppression of those demon spirits that is so thick that you can feel it in the air is what was making David sick!

I went immediately to my room and began to pray. Something came over me in this prayer that I have never felt before in my life. I have prayed in all of our crusades many hours each day, but something in my inner being felt like it just literally was being torn apart.

I began to travail and call out certain things by name. I began to bind them in the Name of Jesus. I began in the Name of Jesus to bind those powers of the enemy—the spirits of sin, the spirits of sickness, the spirits of false religion, the false cults, the spirits of idol worship, and the false prophets of Baal. I found myself binding the power of Satan controlling the religious leaders that might use their influence to try to destroy the crusade!

I was binding these things for hours in the Spirit, not really understanding what I was doing. In that prayer I was loosing the spirit of salvation, and loosing the spirit of healing. When I went out to that meeting, there was no battle to be fought. It was already won! The spirit of salvation was upon those people, and all I had to do was make a little simple approach and they were willing to receive Jesus Christ as their personal Lord and Savior.

You see, something had happened in the spirit world, and that is what brought the flow of the miracle power. The power of darkness that was oppressing and controlling the people was bound! The salvation spirit was loosed. The healing spirit was loosed.

FINNEY'S TRAVAIL

Have you ever read the life story of Charles Finney? If you have not, read it. He was a man mightily used of God in the United States of America. This Congregational minister, a converted lawyer, became president of Oberlin College in Ohio. He had one of the most brilliant minds of his time.

When Finney would go to a city to preach, he would first go into the woods to pray. When he prayed, he entered into an experience of travail and intercession. It would be with unutterable groanings. He did not want to be around anybody because he would pray with such groanings and moanings. It would sound like he was tearing himself to pieces as he would travail in the Holy Spirit for the sins of the people of a community.

WHAT WAS THE RESULT?

After his season of intercessory prayer and travail for

God to move upon a city, he would begin to conduct meetings in a school house, church, or town hall. Soon he was being called to the factories because the spirit of conviction was so strong upon the workers that they would just fall out under the power of the Holy Spirit right on their jobs in the mills. They were being slain in the Spirit under great conviction of sin.

The machines would have to be stopped because there was danger of serious accidents taking place under these conditions.

Soon the bars, houses of prostitution, and theaters would begin to close because the whole town was being converted to Christ.

A NEW VIEW

We went through that whole campaign in India without one problem.

About the fourth day of the crusade God spoke to me and said, "Son, can you see it?"

"Can you see that as soon as you begin to use the same keys to victory in North America that you are using here, the sooner you will see the same anointing in North America?"

I realized that the key that I sought was in my hands all the time.

Sin is sin, evil is evil, demon power is demon power whether it is found in the human cesspools of Calcutta, or in a luxurious apartment on Fifth Avenue in New York City.

Why would we deal with sin in different ways in different places?

It was like my entire being was illuminated, glowing with the light of the Holy Spirit.

I often tell people now that it was the first time in my life since I received Christ at the age of 14 1/2 that I actually saw "the backside of the devil."

This is the side of Satan you see when he is running from you. Yes, I could see him on the run. I now realized that there was no difference in the battle on the foreign fields or right here in North America.

The same key to victory that had shook countries overseas would bring the victory here at home. The spiritual warfare was the same everywhere.

THE SILENT MAJORITY

In North America we had become a silent majority...we never raised our voices, we never lifted a finger while from the comfort of our living room we watched, in living color on television, the rioters burning down our cities, the students tearing apart our educational system, drugs destroying the minds and lives of our young people, the occult making deep inroads into our high schools and junior high schools, crime and lawlessness mounting to record levels, alcohol, divorce, pornography tearing our society apart.

Yes, we stand and watch it, feeling that it is just part of history and we are powerless to do anything about it.

We have been talking about national problems, but the same parallel is true in your personal life and the lives of your loved ones.

I have good news for you. You don't have to sit and watch with that helpless feeling. You have within you the potential power to raise a standard against the enemy and repossess that which he has taken from you.

You can enter into prayer victories never before experienced.

THE BEST DEFENSE

You have heard it said, "The best defense is a good offense." This is so true in the spiritual realm.

The Bible says, *"When a strong man armed keepeth his palace, his goods are in peace: But when a stronger than he shall come upon him, and overcome him, he taketh from him all his armour wherein he trusted, and divideth his spoils." (Luke 11:21,22)*

God is telling us that when Satan, the strong man, keeps people captive with habits, lusts, problems, unsaved loved ones, his goods are in peace; nobody bothers him and the soul is lost for eternity. But when a stronger than he shall come upon him (that is Jesus, Who is greater than Satan), He shall overcome him, and shall take from Satan all his spiritual power (his armor wherein he trusted, and then Jesus will divide the spoils (set the captives free).

The Bible says of Jesus that *"having spoiled principalities and powers, he made a shew of them openly, triumphing over them." (Colossians 2:15)*

God is taking us from a defensive warfare to an offensive warfare.

Paul tells in *Romans 8:38,39* that neither powers nor principalities can separate us from the love of God. We know that Paul didn't just sit back and take a defensive stance against the enemy either; we know by the Bible that he took an offensive one.

He said, *"Take...the sword of the Spirit, which is the word of God." (Ephesians 6:17)* Paul was not about to sit down and let the devil take over.

VIETNAM PARALLEL

I was privileged, at the height of the war in Vietnam, not only to visit that country and minister to the troops, but also to talk with the then commanding officer of all the U.S. forces in Vietnam, General William Westmoreland.

He told me exactly what the U.S. policy in Vietnam was at that time.

Without making a moral judgment on the rightness or

wrongness of that war, let me use this discussion as an example for teaching purposes, because it is so clearly a parallel to the approach most Christians use in dealing with their enemy, Satan.

General Westmoreland told me that the purpose of the effort of the U.S. Armed Forces in Vietnam was not to pursue an enemy and win a military victory or defeat the enemy. Their main purpose was to conduct a defensive war and hold the ground against the invasion of the enemy while training the Vietnamese to be self-sufficient.

They were not to attack the enemy, so to speak, but only to defend themselves when the enemy attacked them. The enemy came in and struck great offensive blows against them, killed and destroyed our men, and then retreated beyond their borders and prepared to attack again. We were never allowed to pursue the enemy beyond a certain point, that is what we called "their territory" as opposed to "our territory" which we were trying (but failing) to defend.

ALL TRUTH IS PARALLEL

What a parallel we have here to the Church and of Christians as individuals.

We have set up a line of defense, and have not even fortified or dug trenches around the territory we do hold. We are doing nothing to prevent the enemy from coming into our lives, conquering our lives and the lives of our children.

We have to destroy the enemy before he destroys us. We have to switch from a purely theoretical (and by nature, impractical) defensive war to an offensive war. We have to go deep into the heart of the enemy's territory with our spiritual warfare, locate him and bind him over the affairs of our lives, our needs, our families, our cities, our country.

The Bible says that Christ, through death destroyed

him who had the power of death, that is, the devil. *(Hebrews 2:14)* and, *"For this purpose the Son of God was manifested, that he might destroy the works of the devil." (I John 3:8)*

This is our purpose as Christians, to go into the devil's territory and invade his stronghold, and take the spoil.

John the Baptist said, *"The axe is laid unto the root of the trees." (Matthew 3:10)* But too many Christians spend their time picking at the branches and the leaves (the outward appearances of the problem) instead of laying the axe of the Holy Spirit, the sword of the Spirit which is the Word of God, to the root of their spiritual problems, the power of sin, sickness, and the devil that binds their spiritual lives.

CHRISTIANS ARE PRUNED BY GOD, BUT SIN MUST BE DESTROYED

The Holy Spirit deals with us in our Christian experience and prunes out the unfruitful works in our lives through various trials and tribulations! But do not confuse this pruning process of the Holy Spirit, which causes us to be more fruitful Christians, with the power of sin and spiritual wickedness which binds many of our lives, our loved ones, and is the root cause of defeat.

Sin is not to be gently pruned away. **It must be cut out at the roots.** If you gently meddle with sin, it will flourish: **you must, through the power of the Holy Spirit, let God destroy it.**

SATAN'S NUMBER ONE OBJECTIVE: DIVISION

Satan recognized a spiritual principle that God set forth in His Word far more than most Christians do. The Bible tells us, *"...the devils also believe, and tremble." (James 2:19)* I am so sorry to say that they have more faith than some of us Christians.

In *Deuteronomy 32:30* we read, *"How should one chase a thousand, and two put ten thousand to flight..."*

Satan realizes the power which comes as a result of unity among God's people. Satan's first priority then, in this spiritual warfare, is to divide the Church.

COMMON GROUND

In a marriage, when the husband and wife start fussing and fighting over little details, their attention will be distracted from how much they hold in common, the love between them, which is most important. That marriage will soon end in separation or divorce.

God has given us, the Church, enough common ground to stand upon: our love for each other and of Christ. We can stand together and leave the rest alone. We must not let our attention get distracted from that common bond of peace between us. We must, as Paul tells us, be *"Endeavouring to keep the unity of the Spirit in the bond of peace." (Ephesians 4:3)*

We do not understand everything, and we do not have all the answers, but I tell you, leave special doctrines alone and be happy in the knowledge that when you get to heaven, God will reveal all things and make it right. The Bible tells us, *"For now we see through a glass, darkly; but then face to face...." (I Corinthians 13:12)*

When I talk about the basics we are united upon, I mean:

1. Believing in your heart and confessing with your mouth that Jesus Christ is Lord, and that God has raised Him from the dead on the third day. *(Romans 10:9,10; I Corinthians 15:4)*
2. That the Blood of Jesus Christ, His Son, cleanseth us from all sin *(I John 1:7)*
3. Baptism in water *(Acts 2:38)*
4. Divine healing *(I Peter 2:24; James 5:14,15)*

5. The Baptism of the Holy Spirit *(Acts 2:4)*
6. The resurrection of all believers, living and dead *(I Thessalonians 4:17)*
7. The Second Coming of Christ *(Acts 1:11)*

These seven points are enough for us to agree upon so that we can have fellowship one with another.

PREPARE FOR BATTLE

When talking about spiritual warfare with satanic forces. you better realize that you are not dealing with a novice. You are dealing with a general of the highest rank.

To go unprepared against the devil is certain defeat, if not spiritual suicide.

Overconfidence or a miscalculation of your own strength will lead to disaster as well.

Humility is one of the most important parts of your spiritual character, for nothing will lead you to certain defeat faster than the attitude that you have the strength and spiritual depth to fight the battle.

This does not mean we live in fear of falling, but it does mean that our dependence is not in our strength and ability but in the Lord.

I can spot the so-called spiritual giants in every one of my crusades. They are the ones who can sit through the moving of the Holy Spirit and walk out of the auditorium exactly the same way they came in, with physical, emotional and spiritual needs.

There is a danger in revelation that a man can become puffed up because God has given him some great truth that others do not possess and then somehow feel he is better and closer to God, more in His favor than others.

Such men forget that the greater the truth and revelation that we possess, the more we become the servants of our fellow Christians, as Jesus said; *"Whosoever will be chief among you, let him be your servant." (Matthew 20:27)*

GET THE BEAM OUT OF YOUR OWN EYE FIRST

This revelation does not give you qualifications to go around with a critical spirit and see what is wrong with your pastor, your church, your brethren and your family. This is a message of love and liberty, not of condemnation and bondage.

If you will be honest with yourself and with God, stop for a moment right now and think of all the inner conflicts you have been having—mental torture, doubt, fears, habits, how you have tried and tried to get the victory over certain things in your life, but it just didn't come.

After a while you gave up, and said to yourself, "Well, I guess this problem is just something I will have to live with the rest of my life." You let the devil deceive you claiming this problem is your thorn in the flesh and God is keeping you "humble." You may have been trying for years to be set free from lust of various sins of the flesh not knowing it is Satan keeping you from being victorious in Christ.

And it does not have anything to do with another super-spiritual excuse, "We are just in the flesh on the face of the earth. We will have to live with these things and not worry about them. If you fall once in a while and sin, don't let it bother you because everybody does it."

Have you forgotten about the Christ Whom the Bible says, *"For he hath made him to be sin for us, who knew no sin; that we might be made the righteousness of God in him." (II Corinthians 5:21)*

I am not saying there is no forgiveness, for the Bible also says, *"If we confess our sins, he is faithful and just to forgive us our sins, and to cleanse us from all unrighteousness." (I John 1:9)* Sometimes, hard as we try, we may fall and commit a sin, but we always must strive against sin and not plan and make provision for it in our minds by twisting the Scriptures to suit our own understanding.

If you will stop for a moment, and be completely honest, you will confess frankly that you really want to be delivered, you really want to be set free, you want control over these things, if only there was a way for it to happen.

Beloved, *"...with God all things are possible."* *(Matthew 19:26)* These things, some of which you buried long ago in your life (and I do not mean buried under the blood) are keeping you from prayer victories in your own life and keep you from reaching the lives of your unsaved loved ones.

THE GOOD NEWS: YOU CAN HAVE THE VICTORY!

God said to me, "Son, the sooner you realize you are not dealing with things but you are dealing with spiritual conflicts, the sooner you will have the victory. You are not wrestling against flesh and blood (you are not wrestling against men), but against principalities and powers and spiritual wickednesses in the high places (you are wrestling against the devil)."

The tip of an iceberg is only about ten percent of the iceberg; it is the only part that we see above the water. The other ninety percent lies beneath the surface. What we have been seeing, and trying to deal with in the spiritual world, is only the surface, the tip of the iceberg, the ten percent that showed. The other ninety percent, the root of the problem, the bondage of demon power, lies beneath the surface of every spiritual problem.

In natural warfare it is not enough to be prepared for battle. You must not only have the desire to go in and defeat your enemy, you have to know how to locate your enemy.

You can have the atomic bomb in your pocket, but if you don't know where to set if off, it will do you no good.

One of the great tactics of warfare is decoys, mock targets that are placed in the field to confuse the attacking army. Your enemy would like to divert the power that you have in Christ to mock targets that really do not mean anything.

The revelation of the New Anointing has shown us where our targets really are. **We are no longer just cutting off the branches of the tree of sin, we are laying the axe to the roots.**

Chapter 9

LOCATING YOUR ENEMY

The world today is in a cup of trembling.

Our politicians, our sociologists, and our psychologists gave the world 10 years (and that was several years ago). Our nation is scared. The world is scared. That fearful looking after that Jesus prophesied of in *Luke 21* has come. People possess a fearful outlook concerning the things that are to come upon the face of the earth.

Air: They are afraid we will not have enough clean air to breathe in the next five or 10 years.

Water: They are afraid all our water systems will be so polluted that we will not have fresh, clear water to drink anymore.

Food to eat: There are already many shortages of food throughout the world and predictions of famine are ominous.

The bleakest part of all this is that sin is rampant and evil is with us on an unprecedented scale.

God spoke these words to me: "There are spirits loosed that have been assigned the devilish task of tearing down the structure and society of this nation, and the sooner

you realize you are not dealing with men or with political
ideologies, the sooner you will have the victory."

WHAT IS THE CAUSE?

There are spirits that are loose in the world.

Somebody said to me, "Brother Cerullo, we don't
mention that word 'spirits' in our church anymore
because my minister says we are not to scare the people."

DEFINING THE ENEMY

**How can you fight an enemy you have not
marked: how can you fight an enemy you close your
eyes to and pretend does not exist?**

A person came to me and said, "Aren't you afraid,
Brother Cerullo, if you talk about spirits people are going
to begin to see things in the air?" I said to him, "If those
things are there, they had better see them!"

There are spirits that are loose in the world. These
spirits have been given the diabolical assignment of
tearing down the structure, the foundation of this
nation—the Constitution, the Bible, prayer, and
everything that is holy.

If every minister, layperson, mother and father had
known what I am talking about, you would have saved
yourselves the chaos and the agony you went through
with your children. If you had only understood the secret
of what I am talking about.

We must realize that we are not dealing with men, and
we are not dealing with political ideologies. I have no
axe to grind with communism. You say, "Why, Brother
Cerullo?" Because to me, communism is a defeated
enemy.

My warfare is not with men. It is not with the social system of our day. It is not with political ideologies.

We are not in a natural battle; we are in a spiritual conflict.

The Scriptures tell us, *"For we wrestle not against flesh and blood, but against principalities, against powers, against the rulers of the darkness of this world, against spiritual wickedness in high places." (Ephesians 6:12)*

CONFUSION

There is confusion over our nation. There is hardly one political leader who will stand up and agree with another on any subject, whether it is on economics, sociological problems, foreign policy, or anything else. There is rampant confusion among our leaders...

Confusion is a spirit.

This spirit of confusion is in the religious world as well, in denominations and even in the lives of believers.

FEAR

There is fear in the atmosphere on an unprecedented scale. Fear is a spirit.

FRUSTRATION

There is total frustration. I was told recently by a leading person in the financial world that presidents of the banks of this country were afraid of what is going to come economically and they are trying to sell their holdings to European and foreign interests. I do not say that to scare you. I say that to let you know the total, hopeless frustration that exists on the highest level of the intelligentsia.

Frustration is a spirit.

PROMISCUOUSNESS

Promiscuousness exists in the air—the atmosphere. There is the relaxing of our moral and our spiritual standards to the point that it is no longer considered immoral to sell the worst kind of literature openly on the streets of this nation.

Now two boys can walk into a courtroom in this country and demand a marriage license to be married as husband and wife. The "gay liberation" of homosexuality and lesbianism receives mass television and press exposure to propagate their codes of conduct to our nation. There are an estimated fourteen million homosexuals in North America.

It is a spirit. Don't fool yourself. It is a spirit of promiscuousness.

These are evil spirits that are loose in this country! This is what God revealed to me in my hotel room in India.

The sooner we realize, as servants of God and as the Church of Jesus Christ, that we are not dealing with men or ideologies, the sooner we are going to have the greatest victory this world has ever seen in the Name of Jesus.

We are not in a natural conflict, we are in a spiritual conflict, and it cannot be solved by Washington, D.C., by religious or political gimmicks, or by any natural means. It must be met, and it can only be met by men and women who have power with God and with men and women who can prevail.

When you really absorb this revelation, you will have some solid understanding beneath your feet that will give you the power to march forward and to know in Whom you have believed.

Your life will never be the same.

"Finally, my brethren, be strong in the Lord, and in the power of his might. Put on the whole armour of God,

that ye may be able to stand against the wiles of the devil." (Ephesians 6:10,11)

THEY ARE LOOSE

The spirits of rebellion, confusion, frustration, turmoil, lust, promiscuousness, sin, dope, unconcern, selfishness, criticism, fear, and anxiety are all loose in our country.

North America has opened the door to all these spirits.

Some of our modern-day Christians are so confused that they do not know the will of God. They do not know where to go; they do not know what to do; they do not know where to turn. They just do not know what decision to make.

Parallel that frustration and that confusion with the confession of the Apostle Paul who said, *"I know whom I have believed, and am persuaded that he is able to keep that which I have committed unto him against that day."* *(II Timothy 1:12)*

"Who shall separate us from the love of Christ? shall tribulation, or distress, or persecution, or famine, or nakedness, or peril, or sword? Nay, in all these things we are more than conquerors through him that loved us." (Romans 8:35,37)

Yes, steadfastness is a spirit also.

As evil is a spirit, good is a spirit.

As hate is a spirit which has infiltrated and ruled this nation and the world, so love is a spirit.

As frustration and confusion are spirits, so is steadfastness.

SICKNESS IS A SPIRIT

Sickness is a spirit. It is a result of the curse. God never intended for man's eyes to become dim or his ears to become weak or even for him to lose his hair.

God intended for man to live forever. He never intended for man to die. Through disobedience the spirit of sin came into the world and as a result, the spirit of sickness.

SALVATION IS A SPIRIT

There are many pastors who will testify that they cannot understand what happened. They may have preached a message to their church that had nothing to do with people getting saved, but suddenly they gave an altar call and people came and received Christ. Then for three, four, or five weeks in a row people kept getting saved. Somehow the spirit of salvation was loosed.

HEALING IS A SPIRIT

The same thing could be said of healing. There have been times when there have been two or three services in a row when there seemed to be a special anointing for divine healing in a church. And then it was like someone shut it off. The preacher did not bring it. He did not create it; he did not seem to especially teach on it. It just seemed to come.

Healing is a spirit.

ALL TRUTH IS PARALLEL

Let us go back for a moment to the story of the woman at the well in Samaria. There is another vital truth in this great story that we need to focus on. When Jesus asked the Samaritan woman for a drink of water, she had a little trick question all ready for Him. Likely it was a cliche of the day...it was the conundrum that no man before could ever answer satisfactorily: "Tell me this if you are a prophet. You Jews say that we ought to worship God at the Temple in the city Jerusalem. We Samaritans say that you ought to worship God in this mountain. You have been able to tell me all about my life and that I am living with a man that is not my husband, can you tell me where I am supposed to worship?" *(John 4:7-20)*

Jesus had the answer.

He looked at her and said, *"God is a Spirit." (John 4:24)* He is not confined to a stained glass window, a robed choir, or the stone architecture of your cathedral, nor to the historic mountain before you.

"God is a Spirit: and they that worship Him must worship Him in spirit and in truth." (John 4:24)

"The hour cometh, and now is, when the true worshippers shall worship the Father in spirit and in truth: for the Father seeketh such to worship him." (John 4:23)

Yes...Say it! God is a Spirit!

GOD IS A SPIRIT

The Bible says that man is created in the image of God. Take a good look at yourself in the mirror. Do you think God looks like you, or like Morris Cerullo? Of course not.

Then where is the image of God if not in our physical features?

In our spirits!

The image of God is within us.

Three things God never intended for man to possess are sin, sickness, and death.

But because man was in God's spiritual image, God had given him a right of choice.

God did not create man as a puppet with strings to pull to make him walk or talk or to love. Man, being in God's image, had the right to choose.

Tragically, he made a wrong choice. Because of Adam's sin of disobedience in the Garden of Eden, because man listened to Satan in the first place, he fell heir to Satan's rewards...sin, sickness, death.

God had said, *"In the day that thou eatest thereof (of the tree of the knowledge of good and evil) thou shalt surely die." (Genesis 2:17)*

Adam did not die physically on that very day, but he died spiritually. Now we are told that *"in Adam all die." (I Corinthians 15:22)* But that same verse tells us also that *"in Christ shall all be made alive."*

So in Christ we are reborn spiritually.

It is the spiritual part of man that is in God's image.

Man is not his physical body. That goes back to the dust. It is the spirit that is you, that will live on through eternity.

Man is spirit.

Now, God is Spirit.

And *Ephesians 6:12* says, *"For we wrestle not against flesh and blood, but against principalities, against powers, against the rulers of the darkness of this world, against spiritual wickedness in high places."*

Satan also is spirit!

The first rule of battle is this: Locate your enemy. We are not in a natural conflict in our problems, our sicknesses, our anxieties, our fears, and frustrations.

We are in a spiritual warfare **in the spirit world**, which is the root cause of all our needs.

LET'S TELL IT LIKE IT IS

Whenever I speak to people today and tell them that many of the problems they are having in their lives are the results of the spirits of Satan, the reaction I usually get is, "Brother Cerullo, are you going off the deep end, and saying that every problem is a demon, or the result of the activities of demons?" No, I am not saying this.

Let's take the mask off. If you walk by a pond and see a fowl with a beak, swimming on the pond, and the sound that comes out of that fowl's beak is "quack, quack, quack," common sense tells us what that fowl is. It's a duck.

Why do you call it a duck? Because it looks like a duck, swims like a duck, and acts and sounds like a duck.

I am not going to tell you that all things that plague mankind today are the results of demons, but if it acts like demon power, do not be afraid to call it exactly what it is.

IGNORANCE BRINGS FEAR

Most people are afraid to identify the work of demon power for what it is. They do not have any idea how to deal with it. They do not know how to go in and press the battle against the enemy and defeat him. They simply have not been taught.

If we can rationalize, and use our psychology and sociology to call insanity and criminality and perversity an "emotional distress resulting from a maladjusted childhood," or any other popular theory used today to explain and justify the problems which plague our generation, then it can be dealt with in the natural mind. But this approach will never find a permanent cure.

But if we define it for what it really is, a spiritual power (that of Satan) which has gotten into their lives or is influencing their habits, then we can deal with it as spiritual power and go in with the supernatural power of God and destroy the enemy in the Name of Jesus.

MOSES VERSUS WITCHCRAFT

The reality of the existence of evil spirits by which Satan, their prince, carries out his evil work can clearly

be attested to by the witness of Moses. In the law of
Moses, which he wrote from the words which Jehovah
God spoke to him on Mount Sinai, we find a clear
definition of the activity of demons in human life. God
calls this involvement "an abomination," a sin of the
lowest degree. *"When thou art come into the land which
the LORD thy God giveth thee, thou shalt not learn to
do after the abominations of those nations. There shall
not be found among you any one that maketh his son
or his daughter to pass through the fire, or that useth
divination, or an observer of times (astrologer), or an
enchanter (psychic medium), or a witch. Or a charmer,
or a consulter with familiar spirits, or a wizard, or a
necromancer. For all that do these things are an
abomination unto the LORD: and because of these
abominations the LORD thy God doth drive them out
from before thee. Thou shalt be perfect with the LORD
thy God." (Deuteronomy 18:9-13)*

God commanded that anyone who was polluted with
these spirits of abomination should receive the death
penalty. (Christ, of course, took the death penalty for
these sins on the cross. If a person dealing with these
things today will repent, God will forgive this sin and that
person will be saved because Christ has paid the penalty
for sin for all those who believe.)

But the words of Moses prove the existence of evil
spirits; their activity of influence and deception among
men, their ability to communicate with and control
human beings, and the Lord God's absolute hatred of these
things.

Do you think that God would give us laws to warn us
against dangers which are imaginary, as some people
today say evil spirits are? Or would God command the
death penalty for dealing with "imaginary" forces?

When Moses and Joshua lived and led the children of
Israel, they strictly enforced these strong measures
decreed by God against the activity of wicked spirits.

Many people were put to death for dabbling with such powers.

After Moses and Joshua died, much of Israel fell into darkness, brought about by the working of evil spirits as the leaders of the people yielded to temptation. They committed the same sins and idolatry and witchcraft and other sins of the people around them, much like many Christians living in America today. This also is a reason why we Christians today experience so much defeat. We leave ourselves open to these things. God said, *"Keep thyself pure." (I Timothy 5:22)*

When Christ appeared in Israel, He immediately recognized that the spiritual problems of the Jewish people were caused by satanic powers, and He began uncompromisingly to wage war against them.

Moses in the Old Testament was a parallel to Christ in the New Testament.

Moses, the only man who knew God face to face; Christ, the only begotten Son of the Father, Who always stood face to face with God in heaven; each recognized the existence of Satan, hated him with a passion, and destroyed his evil work through their lives and works.

David said, *"Do not I hate them, O LORD, that hate thee? and am not I grieved with those that rise up against thee? I hate them with perfect hatred: I count them mine enemies." (Psalm 139:21,22)*

Moses and Christ both knew the devil's power—but they did not let that stop their walk with God, or their people's walk with God! They waged war against it.

SATAN'S FLOOD

Our Church today is at a critical junction in history. A junction is where two roads cross. The road the Church follows is running into attack by the devil as never before, the road that crosses our road is the devil's power. Are we going to let that stop us? He knows that he has but a short season. There are spirits loose in this nation of ours, and the Church faces a challenge by the devil's power it has never faced before.

Are we going to let Satan stop us?

No, sir! For years, the forces of Bible-believing people stood out in their communities as bright and shining lights, a restraint to the evil that always threatened to take over. Now, "modern thought" has usurped power over our lives to the extent that we find a permissive attitude towards these evil works at every level of education and government. The Board of the American Psychiatric Association ruled that they could "no longer call homosexuality a sickness" because "that would be a moral judgment." What is wrong with moral judgments? The Word of God is God's moral judgment on a sin-sick world, and we must live up to God's standards if we desire to be saved. That is the moral judgement of God.

GOD'S STANDARD RAISED

The God I serve is not only a God of mercy, He is a God of wrath as well. And God is demanding a new standard of holiness among His Church today before the second coming of our Lord.

Yes, times have changed, brother. *"As the days of Noah were, so shall also the coming of the Son of man be...eating and. drinking, marrying and giving in marriage." (Matthew 24:37,38)*

But no Christian that walks in the way of the world shall ever see God. *"Blessed are the pure in heart: for they shall see God." (Matthew 5:8)* This New Anointing message is not only a message of power, it is a message of holiness and purification. *"Purify your hearts," (James 4:8)* the Bible says; and if we want to be vessels of God's power, we have to live up to His standards of purity. *"Be ye clean, that bear the vessels of the LORD." (Isaiah 52:11)*

Friend, God never changes.

The Bible never changes.

Sin is sin, and will always be sin.

The devil will never change, neither will he ever be redeemed and forgiven as some modern religions teach us. The Bible says, *"And I saw an angel come down from heaven, having the key of the bottomless pit and a great chain in his hand. And he laid hold on the dragon, that old serpent, which is the Devil, and Satan, and bound him a thousand years, and cast him into the bottomless pit, and shut him up, and set a seal upon him, that he should deceive the nations no more, till the thousand years should be fulfilled: and after that he must be loosed a little season." (Revelation 20:1-3)*

"Jesus Christ the same yesterday, and today, and for ever." (Hebrews 13:8)

What was the need of the world, ten, fifty, a hundred, two thousand years ago?

It has not changed! The world needs to be saved.

There is something that you possess in your life as a Christian that the devil is deathly afraid of.

It is your ultimate assurance of total victory. I am excited to know as you go on in this revelation that the recognition of this will dawn upon you, and you will have prayer victories never before experienced. Needs in your life and in the lives of your loved ones for which you have not been able to penetrate will be met now as never before!

Chapter 10

A SENSE OF PURPOSE

One of the great demonic spirits that is invading our land in both the secular and church worlds today is the spirit of confusion. From this spirit is spawned a multitude of influences that are invading every area of our society.

More than at any time in the history of the world men and women are really wondering what their purpose is. I don't mean just the down and outer, the one who has lost his way and has become a derelict; I mean those in high position, those whom the rest of the world consider successful. If you were really able to get to their innermost being, you would find frustration, because in spite of the vast knowledge that is available today on the human level, it has failed to touch the spirit of man. The more natural knowledge that man accumulates, the more deserted and dry his spirit becomes.

Today it is not the "failure" who commits suicide. It is the man or woman who has found all of the success this world has to offer and is still empty.

The peace, tranquility, sense of fulfillment that was to

be at the end of the accomplishment trail was not there and the void was greater than ever.

Men and women have lost their sense of purpose.

Satan would like to rob every Christian of his sense of purpose. He would like to bring him to the point of confusion where he will ask what is it all about, where do I fit in, is there any real purpose for my life, what am I doing, am I just spinning my wheels, am I just marking time?

Maybe you have either asked these questions in the past or maybe right at the moment these are things that have been going through your mind.

It is not only the world, the unsaved who are asking "Who am I; where did I come from; where am I going?" Satan has made a greater attempt to bring this confusion into the Christians than into the world...what the world is receiving is just an overflow from this satanic thrust at the Church.

The world has many ways of measuring success: money, fame, power, position, etc.

God has only one measurement. Here it is in the life of Jesus, *"...because I seek not mine own will, but the will of the Father which hath sent me." (John 5:30)*

As Jesus repeated in the Garden of Gethsemane as He faced the cross, *"...nevertheless not my will, but thine, be done." (Luke 22:42)*

In *John 5:30* the key word is *"sent."* Jesus was *sent* by the Father into the world.

Jesus was not an accident of history. He was not the man in the right place at the right time just because of the convergence of social and national events...**He was sent!**

Not only was Jesus sent, He was sent for a purpose. Here is where we begin to dispel confusion if we allow the Holy Spirit to speak to us through this revelation of the New Anointing. It is important for every Christian, every born-again believer in Jesus Christ to fully comprehend this truth. Your life, both here on earth and the eternal life which God has promised, are vitally tied to this truth.

Let me show you why.

What was the purpose that Jesus was sent by God to this earth for?

Was it to work the miracles of God? Yes, but that is not all.

Was it to live a pure, godly life, overcoming all temptation so that He would be the sacrificial Lamb? Yes, but that is not all.

Was it to die on the cross for our sins? Yes, but that is not all.

Was it to receive the stripes on His back that we might have physical healing for our bodies as the prophet Isaiah had declared? Yes, but that is not all.

Was it that He might be resurrected from the dead to overcome the power of death? Yes, but that is not all.

All of these individual accomplishments of the life of Christ are wrapped up in one sentence, *"For this **purpose** the Son of God was manifested, that he might **destroy** the works of the devil."*
(I John 3:8)

Jesus came to invade the kingdom of Satan. He came to take it from him and return it to its rightful owner.

How did Satan obtain his kingdom in the first place?

The Bible tells us very clearly.

The story of the events of the Garden of Eden are so misrepresented in the minds of Christians and the world today. Satan has clearly focused our attention on the apple and the supposedly simple act of disobedience of Adam and Eve.

There is far more.

God gave Adam dominion over the earth. What does

that mean? It means that this was man's kingdom, it belonged solely to Adam and Eve because God gave it to them.

What does Satan accomplish in the temptation? Yes, a wall of partition is set up between man and God, but to Satan this was just an added benefit. His great prize was that he received a kingdom, for no longer were Adam and Eve in the driver's seat. It was Satan.

This was not his first attempt to establish a kingdom. We know from Scripture that he led a rebellion in heaven that caused the revolt of one third of the angelic beings. This tells us they were free to make a choice. They were not and are not heavenly puppets on the end of a string.

But though Satan got a following, he was not successful in establishing his kingdom for we know that he was cast out of heaven.

What he could not do in heaven, he accomplished on earth; he obtained for himself a kingdom.

The Apostle Paul, in the book of Romans, explained it this way, *"Know ye not, that to whom ye yield yourselves servants to obey, his servants ye are to whom ye obey; whether of sin unto death, or of obedience unto righteousness?" (Romans 6:16)*

Theologians have always focused our attention on the act of disobedience which of course is primary, but of almost equal importance is that in the same action there was a display of obedience...obedience to Satan that gave him the keys, the title deed to the dominion of this earth.

Why does Satan go about as a roaring lion seeking whom he may devour? *(I Peter 5:8)* It is because this earth was his kingdom.

Adam and Eve became just like the angels in heaven who rebelled against God...the whole scene was re-enacted right here on this earth!

God sent Jesus here for a purpose...to take back the kingdom of this earth from Satan and restore it to its rightful owner.

Some Christians are prone to take Satan quite lightly.

They glibly say that greater is He that is in us than he that is in the world. *(I John 4:4)* I believe that Scripture with all my heart, but I also believe that it takes more than repeating it from memory to make it real.

How great is the Lord in your life? I know how great the Lord is, but only you and the Lord know how great He is in your life. In other words, what real part of you does He have? Twenty percent, fifty percent, seventy-five percent, or one hundred percent?

Why are Christians so buffeted about by Satan? Because the Lord has really not become the greatest part of their life.

Am I afraid of Satan? No! But I will be quick to point out that I have a great deal of respect for his power.

That may shock some of you who have been taught that Satan is powerless, he is only bluffing his way through and only if you believe he has power can he have any influence over your life.

Any being in this universe who has or had the power to draw one third of the angels after him in rebellion is a powerful influence.

The most convincing factor of the reality of Satan's power is the way that God dealt with him.

Consider for a moment the fact that God did not raise up a normal man, a prophet, He **sent** His only Son to "destroy" the kingdom of Satan.

Now let us ask another question. When God sent Jesus to take back the kingdom from Satan, do you believe that He sent Him with the power and the might to accomplish His mission?

We must conclude that, first, God knew the power of Satan and that when He sent Jesus, He gave Him the power and the necessary tools, the weapons of spiritual warfare to win the battle.

Every time that Jesus healed the sick, every time He cast out a demon, every time He performed a miracle, He was invading Satan's territory. I believe that Satan cringed every time a withered arm was made whole.

Every time a blind eye was opened he agonized for he felt that his kingdom was slipping from him; it was in danger.

Jesus came to work the works of God on this earth and the Gospel reveals to us there were two main ways in which He did it: One, the people came by faith to Jesus and took the answer to their need.

Two, Jesus spoke the word and it came to pass.

The centurion soldier came to Jesus and his need was for his sick servant. Jesus indicated that he would come to his house but the centurion said, "Lord, that is not necessary for I know that you are a man of authority. You don't have to personally come to my house, all you have to do is speak the word and my servant shall be healed." *(Matthew 8:8)*

Jesus spoke the word, and we read that in that very hour a distance away the servant was healed and made completely well. A part of Satan's kingdom was snatched away.

One day Jesus arrived in the country of the Gadarenes on the eastern shore of the Sea of Galilee and he was confronted with the man who lived among the tombs and was possessed of a legion of demons. Now we are even getting closer to the heart of Satan's kingdom. As Jesus approaches, the demons cry out of the man, "Don't torment me!" What an ironic statement. here is the source of all torment crying out for mercy. At the command of Jesus the legion of devils leaves the man and for the first time that anyone can remember, he is clothed in his right mind and his body is also covered. *(Luke 8:26-35)*

You can imagine the mighty protest in hell on that day...but the day is not over...Jesus leaves this scene and He is stopped by Jairus, the ruler of the synagogue. His only daughter is dying and he pleads for Jesus to come to his house.

Jesus attempted to go, but because of the press of the crowd it was almost impossible for Him to get through.

In the midst of that great crowd all of a sudden Jesus stops and asked an incredible question: *"Who touched me?"* *(Luke 8:45)*

A woman with an issue of blood, which probably in our day would be diagnosed as cancer, who was given up by the doctors, told to go home and die, uses what might have been the very last strength she has to press through the crowd for in her heart she knows if she can just get to Jesus, she will be healed.

She is healed, but Jesus stops and wants to make sure she knows how she was healed. He explains to her and to the countless millions like her down through the ages that it was not because she touched Him that she was made whole. He declares to her, *"Thy faith hath made thee whole." (Luke 8:48)*

Satan's kingdom is again shaken.

Now Jesus continues on to the house of Jairus. He is met on the way with the message, "Forget it! Don't waste Your time in coming for You have delayed too long. The girl is already dead...there is nothing that You can do about it."

Apparently in this case Satan was safe...but Jesus said, *"Fear not: believe only, and she shall be made whole." (Luke 8:50)*

"Maid arise!"

"And her spirit came again, and she arose straightway: and he commanded to give her meat." (Luke 8:55)

In hell the atmosphere has changed from desperate to "panic"; it is one thing to heal the sick, but when you start commanding departed spirits to return to their bodies, things are getting serious. The battle is heating up.

Now Jesus' friend Lazarus dies. Satan considers this a real victory in advance for everyone knows that it is sometimes easier for you to have faith for a miracle for someone who is not close to you. Lazarus was His close friend.

Now Jesus, You brought back to life the daughter of Jairus, but now let us see if Your power is for real when it concerns somebody with whom You are emotionally connected.

Couple this with the unbelief of His friends and the sister of Lazarus who said, "Lord, he has been dead for three days. If You roll that stone away from the entrance to his grave, the odor will kill us!"

But Jesus speaks the word...a word that resounds down through the corridors of the universe until it reaches the spirit of Lazarus. Lazarus hears a voice commanding him to come forth...to come forth in his physical body.

We read, *"He that was dead came forth, bound hand and foot with graveclothes: and his face was bound about with a napkin. Jesus said unto them, Loose him, and let him go." (John 11:44)*

That day there was an emergency meeting of the security council of Satan's kingdom and long before the cry "crucify Him" rang through the streets of Jerusalem, it echoed through the demon domain. Can you see the principalities and powers in Satan's kingdom gnashing their teeth in vengeance as they see their kingdom being taken from them.

In their blind rage they conclude that there can be only one answer and that is to kill the Son of God. If that could be accomplished, their kingdom would be secure forever.

In their frenzy they conceive the plan to crucify Jesus.

With bated breath they watch the day-to-day unfolding of their master plan. Satan enters into the heart of Judas. The contract is sealed between Judas and the religious leaders. Satan has filled their hearts with jealousy and fear that their kingdoms are threatened by this man from Galilee and they want Him out of the way as much as Satan.

The tension is mounting. The crucial point is reached in the mob scene before Pilate. What would the crowd do? Would they call for the release of Jesus?

No, the mob hysteria goes according to plan and defies all logic. "Release to us a robber, a thief, so that he can terrorize us again, but crucify that One Who has done nothing but good, Who has healed our broken, diseased bodies, Who has brought our dead back to life again. Kill Him, kill Him, we will not have this good man to rule over us."

Would anything go wrong? Did God have some plan that would spoil their whole plot...things were going too smoothly...not a hitch so far...Jesus is taken into Pilate's judgment hall, He is stripped to the waist and the Roman soldiers begin to beat Him with the "cat-o-nine-tails" until His back is hardly distinguishable as belonging to a human...the crown of thorns is placed firmly upon His brow and the blood begins to trickle down through His eyebrows into His eyes making it difficult to see where He is going.

Now the cross, the instrument of final victory for the forces of evil, is planted upon His shoulders...up the mountain to a place called Calvary.

Even as He is placed upon the cross and His hands and feet are nailed with the giant spikes to the cross, the forces of Satan are not sure...will a legion of angels come and save Him? Will Michael the Archangel himself come down and snatch Him from the cross before His spirit leaves His body?

Not until Jesus exclaims *"It is finished"* is there a sigh of relief in the dominions of satanic power.

SATAN'S GREAT DAY

I can see the devil having himself a great field day when Jesus Christ was buried in the tomb. Down in that big, black, ugly abyss of the throne room of Satan all the demons of hell had been called to worship the devil because Jesus Christ, the Son of God, was dead. He had died on the cross. The devil sat back in his wicked glee and said, "I have conquered the Son of God."

The devil did not know it, but on that first day, second day, and third day the blood of Jesus Christ was ascending to the throne of Jehovah God to make atonement for the sins of the world.

The pattern given to Moses and Aaron in the Old Testament was that the blood from the sacrificial lamb was to be caught in a basin.

On the first Passover when Israel was delivered from the bondage of Egypt (which is in biblical language a type of sin), we see the blood of the sacrificial lamb being caught so that it could be applied to the lintel and the door post of each home. *(Exodus 12:7)*

The sacrifice was not enough; the application of the blood had to take place, or death to the eldest son would have occurred as it did to the Egyptians. Moses commanded the Israelites: *"And ye shall take a bunch of hyssop, and dip it in the blood that is in the basin, and strike the lintel and the two side posts with the blood that is in the basin: and none of you shall go out at the door of his house until the morning." (Exodus 12:22)*

So, the hands of Jehovah, so to speak, had reached down on that cross and caught the blood of Jesus. That blood was rising to the throne room of the Father being presented as an everlasting, once and for all, atonement for the sins of the world.

The sacrifice has been accomplished, but no the application of that blood has to be made to the door of the human heart in order to cleanse it from sin and remove from it the specter of eternal death.

Those who would like to believe the fantasy that once you have had the blood applied to your heart, it does not matter what you do from then on because you are saved once and for all, should look at the fact that Moses told them that even after they had applied the blood to the door post they were not to leave the covering of that house or they would be subject to the same fate as the

Egyptians.

The Old Testament required that the blood be sprinkled upon the mercy seat. *"And he shall take the blood of the bullock, and sprinkle it with his finger upon the mercy seat...." (Leviticus 16:14)*

On the third day Jehovah God sent the message down through the corridors of the universe, "I receive the blood of My Son. I receive the blood of My Son."

As it says also in the book of Acts, *"Because thou wilt not leave my soul in hell, neither wilt thou suffer thine Holy One to see corruption." (Acts 2:27)*

A LIGHT

On the third day as this message reverberated from one end of God's creation to the other, something began to happen. A little light began to flicker in the throne room of hell where the great victory orgy was in full swing. That light began to get brighter and brighter until it filled the whole place where Satan and his demons were gathered. Those demons began to scream and cry out like they had never done before because they cannot stand light...their deeds are evil.

The evil came and bowed before that light.

You say, "Brother Cerullo, there is no light in the throne room of the enemy." There was a light there that day! It was the light of the Son of God, because on the third day the devil could not hold Him, the grave could not keep Him, death could not swallow Him up. On the third day He arose, and He walked down into the throne room of the enemy. Why? Because it is written, *"The Spirit of the Lord GOD is upon me...he hath sent me to bind up the brokenhearted, to proclaim liberty to the captives, and the opening of the prison to them that are bound." (Isaiah 61:1)*

The devil bowed before Jesus, but our Lord said, "I have

not come to bind you now, but to fulfill the Word of My Father to give to the Church yet to be born, the victory over all the power of the enemy."

So...with one mighty sweep of victory our blessed Lord reached to the powers of evil, and took from the devil the keys of the kingdom. Then He arose from the grave having opened the prison doors and set the captives free.

Having spoiled principalities and powers He made a show of them "in the back prayer room." He made a show of them "in the quiet counseling room..." Is that what the Bible says?

There are people who want to do everything in secret. I never can understand it. If the Baptism in the Holy Spirit is so good, why do you want to get it in the little private room?

If divine healing is so real and so good, why do you want to get it off in a little corner somewhere?

Here is what the Bible really proclaims, *"And having spoiled principalities and powers, he made a shew of them openly, triumphing over them in it."* *(Colossians 2:15)*

Jesus said, *"Behold, I give unto you power...over all the power of the enemy." (Luke 10:19)*

The devil cannot violate the authority of God which stands behind me. I am a man of authority. The powers of Satan must obey this authority. This is why I say that the devil is a defeated foe. We only need to recognize it!

No, the devil is not afraid of us, but he is afraid of Jesus. He is afraid of the badge of authority that we wear, because we do not stand alone. Behind us stands Jesus. Behind Jesus stands God the Father. With Jesus and God the Father are all the angels and a host of heavenly beings, ready to do the bidding of God Almighty. *"And they went forth, and preached every where, the Lord working with them." (Mark 16:20)*

"And as ye go, preach, saying, The kingdom of heaven is at hand. Heal the sick, cleanse the lepers, raise the

dead, cast out devils: freely ye have received, freely give."
(Matthew 10:7,8)

"Verily I say unto you, Whatsoever ye shall bind on earth shall be bound in heaven: and whatsoever ye shall loose on earth shall be loosed in heaven. Again I say unto you, That if two of you shall agree on earth as touching any thing that they shall ask, it shall be done for them of my Father which is in heaven. For where two or three are gathered together in my name, there am I in the midst of them." (Matthew 18:18-20)

"And Jesus came and spake unto them, saying, All power is given unto me in heaven and in earth. Go ye therefore, and teach all nations, baptizing them in the name of the Father, and of the Son, and of the Holy Ghost: Teaching them to observe all things whatsoever I have commanded you: and, lo, I am with you alway, even unto the end of the world." (Matthew 28:18-20)

Every government on earth or in heaven is guided by a set of rules and regulations. It is those rules and regulations that authorize and empower that government to do the things they do.

In the United States, the operations and functions of our government are based upon the Constitution; if the Constitution does not stipulate a certain thing, the government has no authority to do it.

If America is attacked or threatened in any way, the government has the authority to do whatever is necessary to protect our country; it has the authority, but it must act on that authority and use the power the authority gives it.

Having the authority means nothing unless you use it!

Our government could say to a foreign aggressor, "We have the power and authority to go to war against you," but that will never defeat the enemy unless we go to war.

Satan knows better than most Christians that they have the power and the authority to defeat him, but that does not worry him. Only when he sees them go to war against him does he become afraid.

DOUBLE KEY

"Resist the devil, and he will flee from you." *(James 4:7)* When Satan sees you use the power and authority that you have as a child of God against him, he is not going to stay around for long. He will flee from you!

What is our constitution, the basis of our authority? It is the Word of the living God...the Scriptures, the words of Jesus, His commandments: This is our spiritual constitution!

The devil would like to make you feel like a man without a country, like a person without roots who can be tossed around at will by every different ill breeze that blows, and as long as he can keep you sold on that idea you will never have the victory. *"That we henceforth be no more children tossed to and fro, and carried about with every wind of doctrine..."* *(Ephesians 4:14)*

As a born-again believer, as a child of the living God, you are backed by the greatest Bill of Rights in all of the universe; signed in the blood of Jesus Christ. There is no greater authority, there is no greater power, in heaven or in earth.

DON'T WAIT

This New Anointing revelation teaches how to use this authority and this power in a greater way, but you do not need to wait for that to begin to act!

Our enemy is located! Go to war against him in the Name of Jesus.

For the first time in your life you are going to know what you have to do to win the victory against sin, for unsaved loved ones, for sicknesses, and diseases which have plagued your body for years with no deliverance, for churches whose problems have seemed unsolvable.

This is God's revelation of the decade.

The Church of Jesus Christ has received its marching orders to invade the kingdom of Satan. *"And I will give unto thee the keys of the kingdom of heaven: and whatsoever thou shalt bind on earth shall be bound in heaven: and whatsoever thou shalt loose on earth shall be loosed in heaven."* (Matthew 16:19)

I promise you, you are going to press forward into more prayer victories than you have ever experienced in your life as God makes this revelation real to you.

Not only do we have our enemy located, but also:

We have his complete battle plan...

We know the strength of his power...

We know what it will take to resist him and bring deliverance from all his works...

We know that we have the power and authority of God to back us up.

We have an anti-Satan defense system that he cannot penetrate if we will use it!

Chapter 11

HOW TO MOVE FROM IMITATION TO PARTICIPATION

Begin to lift your shield of faith and wield your sword of the spirit because God is now telling His Church it is time to go to battle. In the study of the history of the Church, certain patterns of the moves of the Holy Spirit become very apparent. It is evident that God moves in cycles.

In many instances the Holy Spirit would bring the revelation of a certain truth that had been dormant in the Church for many years. That revelation would inject new life into the Church and a period of revival to apostolic Christianity would result.

This was the case with Martin Luther. *"The just shall live by faith." (Romans 1:17)* That Scripture was in the Bible in all of the seventeen hundred years that preceded Luther's time from the beginning of the Church, but then it became a new revelation and the Reformation was the result.

The same was true with the other great revivalists such as the Wesleys and Charles Finney.

We are seeing it in our day with a new outpouring of the Baptism of the Holy Spirit that has crossed all denominational lines in a greater way than any previous revival.

Paralleling this move is a greater revelation of the workings of the spirit world. God's people are learning how to cope with and how to overcome those forces that have been assigned by Satan to break the power of God in the life of every Spirit-filled believer.

If you do not consider this a very present revelation that is sweeping the religious world today, consider the statements made recently by Billy Graham confirming his belief in a very real personage of Satan and demon power:

"All of us engaged in Christian work are constantly aware of the fact that we have to do battle with supernatural forces and powers. The devil follows me every day. He tempts me. He is a very real presence to me."

Consider the statements made by Pope Paul concerning the activity and work of Satan in the world today. He emphasized that Satan is not just a symbolic being, but a real force to be reckoned with:

"The smoke of Satan has entered the temple of God through a fissure in the church..."

"Evil is not merely a lack of something—but an effective agent—a living, spiritual being—a terrible reality, mysterious and frightening."

Read the reports in our leading periodicals speaking of the devil as a living spiritual being, and that our greatest need today is to have the ability to effectively cope with his power.

DON'T PRETEND THAT IT ISN'T THERE

Some ministers have been turned off in the past by an over-emphasis on demonic activity. There is the danger of beginning to see Satan in every problem and trouble that arises...**but there is a far greater danger for us to bury our head in the sand and pretend that the devil is not there.**

Some have taken the attitude that it is only necessary to emphasize the positive aspects of the power of God in our life...but that is like training an army of soldiers to go out to war, and never telling them anything about the enemy they are going to face.

We have learned in our day that in the natural there are many kinds of warfare. A small guerrilla type army can in time pick apart and defeat an army hundreds of times larger, if that large army refuses to adapt to the type of warfare it faces.

Satan is a military genius in spiritual warfare. He has at least six thousand years experience in constant warfare. God has not left us, however, as sitting ducks on the pond ready to be picked-off.

The principle that must be understood is the method of operation of God in our lives...if this one principle were fully understood by the Church, it is impossible to comprehend the difference it would make.

NOT TO US OR FOR US BUT THROUGH US

God never does anything **to** us!

God never does anything **for** us!

...but always **through** man!

The **ultimate, greatest intention of God for all of our lives is not that we become imitators, but that we become participators.**

The intention of God is not for our lives to be struggling to be like His, but rather for His life to flow through our beings; not to transform our flesh but that His glory, His life, His light, His power may work in us and through us.

116 THE NEW ANOINTINGTHE NEW ANOINTING

THE WEAPON OF FAITH

"For whatsoever is born of God overcometh the world: and this is the victory that overcometh the world, even our faith." (I John 5:4)

This Scripture, if not correctly interpreted, could lead someone to think that all we have to do is believe something and Satan is overpowered. That interpretation fails to comprehend the meaning of "faith" as used in this Scripture.

First, you must realize that faith is a weapon.

Second, you must fully understand that faith is not an offensive weapon, but rather for defense. In Ephesians it is described as a shield: *"Above all, taking the shield of faith, wherewith ye shall be able to quench all the fiery darts of the wicked." (Ephesians 6:16)*

One of the prime characteristics of a shield as a weapon is that it is of little value lying on the table. This weapon, to have any effectiveness in battle, must be picked up, and not only picked up, but it must be raised in the direction that the enemy is coming from.

The revelation of the New Anointing that has been revolutionizing the lives of thousands of ministers and laymen around the world has pinpointed the position and the method of approach of Satan in our lives.

One of the first things that the Holy Spirit showed us was Satan's battle plan. We now know his strategy and exactly where he will attack.

THE ONLY PLACE SATAN CAN ATTACK YOU!

There is only one place that Satan can attack a man or a woman, whether they are a Christian or have never accepted Christ into their lives.

That one place is in our minds!

The results can be revealed in other areas, but this is the only way for him to attack us.

When we fully comprehend and realize this, then we are able to take that defensive weapon of faith, which is our shield, and use it to protect our minds.

We do not need to worry about an attack coming from any other direction because this is the only path that Satan can take.

When that thought war starts, we can raise the shield of faith against it immediately and defend ourselves from all the onslaughts and fiery darts of the enemy.

It is not an automatic weapon...it has to be raised. Put it into position!

THE GREAT COUNTERFEIT

Satan is so jealous of God that he tries to imitate God in every way. He was created second-in-command only to God Himself. He was the highest angelic being. His brightness and his glory was unequaled, second only to God. He wanted to be brighter and more glorious and more worshiped than God. He wanted first place in the heavenlies. *"For thou hast said in thine heart, I will ascend into heaven, I will exalt my throne above the stars of God: I will sit also upon the mount of the congregation, in the sides of the north: I will ascend above the heights of the clouds; I will be like the most High." (Isaiah 14:13,14)*

We said a moment ago that God will only work through us...Satan has taken his cue, and he also has the objective of working through human agencies.

The Bible says: *"Wherein in time past ye walked according to the course of this world, according to the prince of the power of the air, the spirit that now worketh in the children of disobedience." (Ephesians 2:2)*

Note: *"The **spirit** that now worketh in the **children of disobedience.**"*

What is Satan trying to do? He is trying to counterfeit God, Who never does anything to us or for us...He is always working through us.

YOUR ONE OFFENSIVE WEAPON

It may amaze you to know that God has left you with only one offensive weapon to use in all of your spiritual warfare.

There are two reasons for this:

> One, it is so powerful that you do not need any other and,
> Two, having only one eliminates any confusion about what weapon to use in any given situation.

The Bible says: *"And take...the sword of the Spirit, which is the word of God."* (Ephesians 6:17)
There is no other offensive weapon given to the Christian to fight with except the Word of God!
It is in the use of the weapon where the difference lies.

A CONFESSION

There was a time in my life, not so long ago, that I took the Scripture, *"Greater is he that is in you, than he that is in the world"* (I John 4:4) as an insurance policy for my spiritual well-being and protection. I viewed it as an automatic defense weapon against Satan.

It was my impression that all I needed to do was to stay close to Jesus, and Satan could not touch me. Since then I have found out that things are not exactly that way.

SATAN IS NOT IMPRESSED

In fact, they are just the opposite. The closer I get to Jesus, the more fiercely rage the attacks of Satan.

Some people have the idea that Bible studies make the devil flee. You might be surprised to know how many Bible studies Satan attends.

(NOTE: You must be careful not to read just a portion of the following statements...if you are not going to read it all, do not read any of it.)

Taking your Bible out in a time of crisis and beginning to read and to search the Scriptures does not overly impress Satan.

Bible drills do not make Satan run...in fact, you could memorize the Bible from Genesis to Revelation and that in itself would not move Satan one inch away from your life.

VAIN REPETITION

Scores of people reading this message have attemped to get the victory by just an assimilation of the Word of God. Many are asking in their minds at this point of the message, "Brother Cerullo, what do you mean? How can I memorize the Scripture and it not have an effect on Satan?"

Quoting the Scripture alone will have no effect on Satan...only when that word coming from your lips has been given specific direction toward Satan will it accomplish the task for which it is intended. Otherwise it is empty, entirely devoid of the explosive might of the Holy Spirit.

SELECTIVE AIM

In order for the Word of God to have the explosive might of the Holy Spirit, it has to be taken and personally directed against the attacker.

Do not misunderstand...there is great value in committing the Bible to memory, but that value is only realized and effective if it is used properly...it is not an automatic result! You must raise it...aim it...and fire it!

THE DOUBLE KEY: SUBMIT AND RESIST

The Bible says, *"Submit yourselves therefore to God. Resist the devil, and he will flee from you." (James 4:7)*
You cannot have one without the other!
Here is the double door to victory and the overcoming life. To use just one door will leave you in a spiritual vacuum.

There are people who are correctly resisting the devil, but have never really submitted themselves to God. Therefore, their resistance is not backed by the power of the Holy Spirit in their lives.

Then there is the other group who are constantly submitting themselves to God, but are living the most up-and-down defeated life that anyone could live.

I have personally counseled with thousands of people around the world. They love God. They want to serve God, but can never get the victory. They claim that for one reason or another they do not want to commit this or that particular sin. They have submitted themselves to God...they have yielded their lives to Him...they have spent hours in prayer and travail...but one thing is missing, **they have submitted, but they have not resisted.**

PRESSING THE POWER BUTTON

Until we press the power button, we do not release any action against Satan and that comes not by an inward action (submission)...but by an outward action (resistance).

There are scores of people who submit themselves to God every day of their lives, but fail to resist the devil.

He only flees when you resist...resistance is a word of **action.** It means a fight...it means a battle...and until you engage the enemy in battle he will be right by your side to pick your spiritual life apart piece by piece until you are a spiritual skeleton.

POWER INSTEAD OF PANIC

Too often, instead of pushing the power button of **resistance,** we are pushing the panic button of **fear.** There is no clearer indication to Satan that he has us exactly where he wants us.

HOW TO AMUSE THE ENEMY

When you continue just to practice with your spiritual weapons, all you do is amuse the enemy. As long as you memorize and practice, Satan will feel a great deal of security...but his expression will change as you have the courage to raise that weapon...point it in his direction...and as he looks down the barrel of your spiritual firepower with your finger on the trigger, the urge to flee will overcome him.

I am so glad of that word **flee.** It just does not say that Satan will leave, it says that he will **flee,** and that speaks of a hasty, panic departure.

FAITH IS A FACT, BUT FAITH IS ALSO AN ACT

I do not believe that there is any truth that God has given to me in my ministry that I have repeated so many times to so many millions of people as this simple truth concerning faith.

In God's scheme of things, it appears to me that every provision that He has made requires an action on our part. It is so completely in line with the character of God never to force anything upon us against our will, whether it is good or bad.

In the world of chemicals you always need a catalyst to produce a reaction. Until the catalyst is found, the reactive potential of two chemicals is dormant.

The catalyst of faith is "action."

The revelation of the New Anointing is not confined to any one area of our lives, but is all-encompassing...it is a message to the entire sphere of human endeavor.

I realize as I write this message that the Holy Spirit will cause it to fall into the hands of those who need this revelation.

At this same time, I realize that the principle of action is again in force. I do not believe that you have read this book by accident. The Holy Spirit is desiring to work a special work in your life.

In this book there is knowledge that can unlock prayer power to victories that you never dreamed would ever happen in your lifetime, and yet...that knowledge alone is not enough...the knowledge, the revelation of this message will not do you one ounce of good unless you take **action**.

Let me tell you something that is a tragic fact...unless you act now, there is a ninety percent chance that you will never act.

Why?

Because right now, yes, right this very moment, the Holy Spirit is prompting you...is wooing you...to respond, to act, and if you put it aside, the affairs and the cares of this life will soon choke out the revelation that you have received.

Under the anointing of the Holy Spirit I am going to recommend that you do two things:

One, submit your life, your will, to God **right now.** Submit and commit that need...the need to overcome that habit of tobacco, that need to overcome that lying spirit...that need to overcome that bad temper that has constantly caused you defeat...the need for power to control that tongue that at the least instigation has cut your loved ones to pieces...the need to demonstrate more of the love of Christ to your family...and any other need that you know is in your life right now, physical, spiritual or emotional.

Submit it to God right now.

Two, begin **right now** to direct that sword of the Spirit right to the center of the enemy's attack on your life. Ask the guidance of the Holy Spirit to take the right Word of God to resist the enemy that he might immediately begin his flight.

Chapter 12

A CLOUD OF WITNESSES

Paul said, *"We are surrounded by a cloud of witnesses."* *(Hebrews 12:1)*

That the New Anointing revelation works when put into action is attested to by thousands of witnesses who have had miracle answers to prayer since they put these principles into action. This has been the factor which has led to greater, more miraculous answers to prayer in my own life and ministry in the past several years than ever before in all the years of my ministry. Letters and telephone calls pour into my headquarters in San Diego every day from men and women all across the nation who have found that the New Anointing works! They have applied these truths and their prayers have penetrated into the very spirit world, binding those spirits that are evil and loosing upon their own lives and those of their loved ones the blessings that God intended for them to have.

Through the revelation of the New Anointing God has placed in your hands the potential, the spiritual atomic bomb, to more than defeat every attack of the devil, past, present, and future.

It is not enough to have it in your grasp...you must begin to use it.

When I think of the millions of books written that have the power to lift people's lives to a higher potential yet are just sitting on shelves collecting dust, it makes me realize again how I must depend upon the power of the Holy Spirit to stir people's hearts. Peter said, *"I stir up your pure minds by way of rememberance...." (II Peter 3:1)*

Do not put this book on the shelf until it has accomplished in your life what the Holy Spirit intends it to do. Let Him stir you.

My dear fellow minister, God wants to give you the joy of seeing things happen when you preach and minister. Far more important than what you say is the anointing in which it is said. In our meetings I have seen people receive outstanding miracles of healing and give their hearts to Jesus who were too overwhelmed by the Holy Spirit to understand a word that I said.

The anointing of the Holy Spirit spoke to their hearts. They reached out from their hearts to receive God's salvation, God's healing and miracle-working power in their lives.

There have been times in our services here in North America when I have walked out onto the platform and felt the tremendous power of the Holy Spirit convicting men and women of their sins, calling them to get right with God.

My first question has been, "How many right here in this audience have never had the experience of being born again?" Hundreds of hands have been raised sincerely. They weren't backsliders; they simply had never in their lives received Christ and most of them had never been asked to receive Christ as their personal Savior.

Then in the simplest of terms, taking nor more than five minutes, I would explain the plan of salvation. Without a single emotional story, I would ask them the question, "How many would like to be born again? How many would like to receive Jesus Christ as your personal Savior?"

Within five minutes from the time I stepped to the microphone there would be more than two hundred and fifty people at the altar. Many of them would stand there before me with tears streaming down their faces when five minutes before they didn't even know what it meant to be saved.

I am convinced that the Holy Spirit can do more in one split second than we can do by our efforts in a lifetime.

Pastor, you don't have to walk away from your church after each service with that empty, frustrated feeling, wondering seriously if you should ever go back again. Put the principles of the New Anointing into practice.

This is by no means to discount the need for preparation in prayer and in the Word. Rather, it actually intensifies your desire to be prepared.

In the first service of our Dallas, Texas crusade, I came out prepared to preach a message. I had spent hours in my room in preparation and prayer. As I started to announce my subjects for the next two nights, a woman who had been in a wheelchair for ten years got up and walked down to the altar.

What was I to do? Tell everybody to just hold steady and wait until after I delivered my message to receive their miracle? I really had little choice. I just had to stand back and let the Holy Spirit take over completely.

More and more in our crusades I actually am feeling the part of a spectator because I don't feel responsible for what is taking place. My participation takes place back in my room in using the principles of spiritual warfare that I have described in this book.

When I describe the results of the New Anointing, I am not speaking from belief or theory only and not from just my own life, but from countless testimonials of ministers whose lives and ministries have been completely transformed.

Not long ago, going through customs in Vancouver, British Columbia, I met an Eskimo pastor who told me, "Brother Cerullo, I came to the Portland Crusade and Holy Spirit Teaching Seminar a year ago and my life has never been the same since."

In Tampa, Florida, Rev. Charles Strickland of the Grant Park Baptist Church reported several weeks after the crusade was over that he had not had the opportunity to preach a regular sermon in the past six weeks. In every service the Holy Spirit just completely took over and the Word was coming forth under the inspiration of the Spirit. Miracles and healings were literally shaking the community. The church was in a continual revival and there were immediate plans to triple the size of the sanctuary to accommodate the crowds.

This Baptist church was on fire before the crusade, but it has now literally exploded and still is exploding for God in the Tampa Bay area.

CHURCH EXPLOSIONS

Rev. Jess Jackson of Bethel Temple in Dallas, Texas, described himself as a very conservative man before the Dallas crusade. He reported afterward that he is a new preacher and he has a new church. "You just wouldn't recognize our church!" he exclaimed.

Rev. George Stormont of Manchester, England, is the perfect picture of an England gentleman with stately bearing.

He pastors Beth-Shan Tabernacle in Manchester, one of the largest Spirit-filled churches in the British Isles. After the New Anointing got hold of him he needed a dry set of clothes waiting for him when he finished preaching on Sunday nights. Souls were saved in nearly every service. It wasn't the increased physical effort that produced the result, but the power of the Holy Spirit that was now so much more present in his preaching.

NOT FOR PASTORS ONLY

The New Anointing is not for ministers only. God is not a respecter of persons but looks on the heart, these principles and this authority are for all who enter into the flow of God and claim them.

Rebecca Hager of Denver, Colorado, was a lady who had been bound for years by the need for frequent hormone shots. If Rebecca did not have a shot every ten days, she would become so tense and overwrought that she wanted to kill somebody. She used to send her little children out to play for fear she would kill them in one of these indescribable attacks. The fact that Rebecca was a Christian and loved God made the situation even more unbearable, as she knew this was not in harmony with the fruit of the Spirit she was supposed to exhibit in her life as a child of God. It was very frustrating. Her husband used to watch for the symptoms that told him she needed another shot.

Rebecca also had a number of other problems. She had a growth on her thyroid gland, was allergic to "almost everything," had varicose veins and arthritis. She also had a disabled arm which had been injured during her childhood when she fell from a horse.

Rebecca came to my Holy Spirit Teaching Seminar in Denver and sat through the morning classes, drinking in of God's Presence and the spiritual food lifted her to new spiritual planes. She wasn't even thinking about her physical needs, just basking in the spiritual atmosphere.

On the closing morning of the series I said, "Now we are going to put what we have learned into action. I want every one of you to begin praying. I want you to come against every spirit of Satan which touches your life or those of your loved ones."

As I spoke, Rebecca's hands went up and she began to

exercise this power and authority from God.

She said later, "My mind was a complete blank when it came to knowing what it was I wanted to be loosed from. It never occurred to me I was under bondage to hormones, but I commanded Satan to loosen everything that affected my life."

Immediately she felt the warm flow of God's Spirit in her arm and that disabled arm was loosed. The next morning while washing her face, she discovered that the growth on her thyroid was gone.

It was several days after the conference when her hormone shot was to become due...but not feeling any of the previous symptoms, Rebecca didn't take a shot. One extra day went by, then two, three, four. She waited for her husband to say something, but he didn't. A whole month went by before he asked her one morning, "Isn't it about time for your shot?"

"No I don't take those anymore," she told him, for God had completely loosed her of the need for that medication. She no longer had an urge to kill or attacks of nerves. Through exercising of the New Anointing, she had found out that what she learned in the teaching sessions worked when put to use in her own life. The varicose veins, arthritis and allergies were also healed.

Jean Vickers suffered from one of the worst afflictions known to medical science. Tic Douloureux is sometimes called "Devil's Pain" for good reason. Doctors say that nine out of ten people who reach the advanced stages of the painful disease attempt suicide. The pain and suffering become so intense that everything becomes unreal.

Jean, though a Christian, decided she could not cope with the pain any longer. She went into the garage to hang herself. The noose was all ready. Only a last minute crying out to God from the very depths of her being saved her from this awful act. Still she continued to suffer.

Several months before our crusade in Sacramento, California, the doctors began giving her a powerful new drug that took away the pain but left her in a virtual stupor. She was warned that regardless of the condition of the disease, she would be hopelessly addicted to the new drug.

She attended the crusade services each night and she also came to the morning Holy Spirit Teaching Seminar services. Morning after morning her faith increased. Neither Jean nor I can tell you the exact moment that her miracle happened. On Thursday evening during the message on prophecy, an inner voice told her something was different and that it would not be necessary for her to take her medicine any longer.

There was no mention of healing or prayer for the sick during that service, but Jean went home with an assurance that she was healed of the dread affliction that has baffled medical science.

Her husband warned her that if she did not take the medicine, she would be a raving maniac in the morning. Though in the natural she knew that this was true, she did not take the powerful drug that had been prescribed for her.

When she woke up in the morning, she realized she was totally healed and has never taken that medication since!

FOR THE FAMILY

Mrs. Elsie Parmeland of Ridgewood, New Jersey, is typical of millions of parents across North America and around the world. It should not surprise us that children are growing more and more rebellious. We can point out many things in our society that are contributing factors. However, never forget that the Apostle Paul in describing conditions in the last days before the return of Christ said it would be this way.

Mrs. Parmeland said that her daughter was the most

rebellious child you would ever meet. She hardly ever smiled. If her parents tried to touch her, she would pull away, not allowing any embrace or affection.

"When I stood in that vast auditorium," Mrs. Parmeland later related, "during the last day of your Holy Spirit Teching Seminar in Toronto, with tears running down my cheeks, I put into action the things you had taught us. I bound the spirit of rebelliousness in my child and released the spirit of love.

"When I returned home, my daughter ran to me, threw her arms around me and said, 'Oh, Mother, I missed you. I missed you.' Can you imagine what this meant to me?

"All I could say was 'Praise God, Praise God.'"

Maybe this is the reason that God has placed this book in your hands. The same keys, the same message, the same revelation that Mrs. Parmeland received at the Toronto Holy Spirit Teaching Seminar are in this book.

God is a Spirit and the same New Anointing that broke the rebellious spirit in her daughter will work for the spiritual and emotional needs of your family.

You have the power right now to begin to change things …you are no longer helpless…you no longer just have to stand there and try to take everything that Satan throws at you…resist him through the power of the New Anointing and he will "flee from you."

EVERY AREA OF LIFE

Ten million people in America are now alcoholics. One out of every five cars you meet on the road is being driven by a man or woman under the influence of alcohol. Linda Thomas of Tampa, Florida, and Eileen Smith of Dallas, Texas, both were unable to cope with the realities and pressures of life without a constant flow of liquor. Their greeting to their husbands when they came home at night was to ask them if they had brought another bottle or not.

Both of these ladies suffered physical afflictions as a result of their drinking, but still did not have the power within themselves to quit. Each of these ladies came into contact with the message of the New Anointing and both have been completely delivered from the physical and emotional need of alcohol.

Millions of dollars are spend every month in America on diets: Diet pills, food, drink, doctors, clubs, clinics and what have you to help people curb their appetites.

Just to show you that this revelation covers every area of our lives, I will share with you a letter received from Linda Okerstrom of Downers Grove, Illinois: "I want to praise the Lord for healing me of a compulsive appetite that has caused me untold heartache and suffering ever since I was eight years old. To His glory and honor I can report a weight loss of 25 pounds! I have never been so at peace in my life as far as dieting is concerned."

A lady in Tampa, Florida, had been divorced from her husband for five years. She still loved him and prayed every day for his salvation. He was involved in underworld activities and the conflict in the home became more than she could bear.

She attended the Holy Spirit Teaching Seminar in Tampa and in the first service received enough of the New Anointing revelation to begin to use it. Her objective was her former husband. She began to bind the evil powers that held this man in their grip.

Then she called and invited him to one of the meetings in the evening. He came on Thursday night, and at the conclusion of my message on prophecy, he came to the altar and gave his heart to Jesus.

Another family has been reunited by the power of the Holy Spirit.

From Fresno, California, a lady wrote: "I attended your Fresno Holy Spirit Teaching Seminar, and what a thrill for me! The Lord saved me from fourteen years of dope addiction and demon oppression."

Mrs. Richard Romero of Fullerton, California, wrote this

triumphant testimony: "For the first time in years I've been set free and delivered forever from that filthy cigarette habit. I truly experienced a beautiful victory over them. Not only did He deliver me from the cigarettes. He also removed the terrible desire."

That was similar to the letter form Mr. Lynn Peterson of Watause, Tennessee, who wrote: "I just read your article on "How to Move From Imitation to Participation" and I just quit smoking. I have been praying for the strength to quit and through your article God revealed the strength inside of me through Himself."

A Vermont woman's report is: "I recently wrote asking your advice on how to bring peace into my home. I applied your answer and wish to report that my husband's drinking and cruelty have miraculously ceased."

NEW AREA OF SPIRIT

Mrs. Vada Gamble wrote from Gilman City, Missouri: "My husband and I have found a new area of the Spirit to live in. We have seen our building program begin (a Full Gospel church). We have seen our only son begin to be more involved in His service and found the Lord's will in other things. We have both been wonderfully touched physically and spiritually."

Rev. Louise Henry is pastor of a black church in Brooklyn. Five years ago, she was so ill with a perforated ulcer and other conditions that she was too weak to pastor and the church was ready to close. Louise came to the Regional Deeper Life Conference in Lansing in 1970. She did not receive her healing during the conference, but after she returned home, she prayed out in the Spirit and was miraculously healed. She disposed of all her medicine and went into the kitchen to prepare herself a steak dinner, although doctors had said her diet would be baby food for the rest of her life. She was also healed of an obscure disease called Christian Webber disease which caused large egglike nodules to grow all over her legs, and for which doctors had found no cure.

But that is not all. She plunged into her pastoral duties with new strength and the New Anointing. A few months later her congregation had bought a new church complex which opened with 300 people present and Louise conducts a regular television program called the "God Answers Prayer" program.

Regarding not only her miraculous healing but the flourishing church congregation, Louise said, "I started using the faith principles you taught me."

Not just from America, but also from many countries around the world, testimonies pour in. Men and women of God, who used to have "good" ministers, have seen their effectiveness multipled.

So you see, we have a great cloud of witnesses.

As you have read this book you have been surrounded with a cloud of witnesses to the fact that God wants to meet your need right now and that He is able to meet that need, whatever it is.

I am a firm believer that nothing in life happens by chance. I don't know how this book came into your hands. Maybe you ordered it, maybe it came as a gift, maybe someone has loaned it to you, or maybe you have no idea how it happened to come into your possession.

I do know that the message that it contains will revolutionize your life if you will let it.

"If you will let it..." Isn't it strange that the God of the universe Who created by His mighty power all that we can see and the vast universe beyond, isn't it strange that just His spoken Word cannot make you use the power and blessing that He has provided to meet your need?

IT IS UP TO YOU

It is up to you...It is in your hand...I have brought the message face to face to thousands of people.

I do two things: One, I deliver the revelation that God has given to me under the anointing of the Holy Spirit. I believe that you can feel that anointing as you read this book.

Two, at the end of every School of Ministry I pray for each one who has attended that they shall not only be hearers of the Word, but doers also...that the message that they have received shall cause them immediately to see the results of this message in their lives.

I pray that every one who reads this book shall become more than a conqueror in Christ, but I want to go one step further...I want to pray specifically for you...pray for you by name and pray for your specific need.

Only you can allow me to do this by writing me a letter and telling me the areas of your life that need the power of the New Anointing to break the power of sin or sickness.

If you will write me, I promise you that I will personally pray for your need and I will write you back with the answer God gives me for your need.

You can receive the New Anointing right there in your home. You can begin to use it to put Satan to flight and win the biggest victories you have ever known in your whole life.

I am waiting for your letter that I may more effectively pray for your needs. Let me hear from you.

Most of all I want God to give you a New Anointing in your life...and bring you now, in prayer, victories you have never before experienced.

Use the coupon on the last page of this book and mail it in to me today!

Morris Cerullo World Evangelism • P.O. Box 85277 • San Diego, CA 92186-527

Morris Cerullo World Evangelism of Canada
P.O. Box 3600 • Concord, Ontario L4K 1B6

Morris Cerullo World Evangelism
P.O. Box 277 • Hemel Hempstead, HERTS HP2 7DH, England

PERSONAL REVELATIONS GOD HAS GIVEN ME FOR MY LIFE AS I READ THIS ANOINTED MESSAGE:

AREAS OF BREAKTHROUGH IN MY LIFE THAT I AM BELIEVING GOD FOR:

I AM TAKING AUTHORITY OVER SATAN IN THE LIVES AND NEEDS OF THESE FRIENDS AND LOVED ONES:

ANSWERS TO PRAYER THAT CAME AS THE RESULT OF THIS "NEW ANOINTING" IN MY LIFE:

Experience the Presence and power of God on this "New Anointing" revelation truth!

Hear Morris Cerullo as he presents this dynamic message under the anointing of the Holy Spirit...recorded live just as Morris Cerullo taught it at the School of Ministry!

Now available in a special six-tape audio cassette package...you will be able to receive the full blessings of God to transform your life into a new dimension (all six tapes are C-90s, over nine hours of anointed teaching by Morris Cerullo, recorded live in a School of Ministry session.)

Use this teaching tape series in your home for Bible study and prayer meeting groups as well as in your church. This album also makes an ideal gift for a friend or loved one.

This complete six-tape set, packaged in a beautiful album, is yours free for a love gift of only $30 or more...a seed gift to help train National ministers to reach their nations for Christ.

If purchased separately these tapes and album would cost $52.95. As a special offer, only available through the album can be yours for a love gift of only $30 (U.K. £18, Canada $38).

Enclose your gift check or money order with the request form at the back of this book and mail in today.

MORRIS CERULLO WORLD EVANGELISM

U.S.:
P.O. Box 85277
San Diego, CA 92186

U.K.:
P.O. Box 277
Hemel Hempstead HERTS HP2 7DH

CANADA:
P.O. Box 3600
Concord, Ontario L4K 1B6

Website: mcwe.com
Email: morriscerullo@mcwe.com

I want to pray for you...for a New Anointing on your life, your family and your ministry!

What ever your needs are today, I want to agree with you in prayer and take them to the throne of God so you can experience a miracle! This will build your faith to believe God for even greater miracles as you apply these New Anointing principles to your prayer life! "...if two of you shall agree on earth as touching any thing that they shall ask, it shall be done for them of my Father which is in heaven." (Matthew 18:19)

☐ You will receive a new spiritual anointing on your life, family and ministry!

☐ You will experience a new spiritual breakthrough that will take you past surface knowledge and enable you to meet all your needs...at the root cause!

Write out your prayer needs right now on the tear-out coupon at the end of this book and mail it to me today!

I want to send you this New Anointing prayer cloth!

I feel moved by the Holy Spirit to challenge you to take a special step of action...a step of faith! If you want the New Anointing power to come upon your life, let me send you this prayer cloth. Since I cannot be there in person to lay hands on you to receive a greater anointing from God, I will anoint this simple cloth with oil (oil is a type of the Holy Spirit) and will pray over it so it can become a point of contact for your faith as we agree together in prayer.

I promise you...God will honor your step of faith and you will experience a new spiritual breakthrough of power in your life!

There is a greater anointing upon me now than ever before to pray for your needs.

Never before, in my more than 56 years of frontline ministry have I carried a deeper burden for the Body of Christ than I do now.

I have prayed, fasted, interceded, agonized and fought spiritual warfare against satanic powers...

...and God gave me a vision!

God said..."Place the needs of my people upon the altar before My Presence...Jesus is praying for all their needs to be met!"

A vision of Jesus Christ, our Great High Priest, praying for all your needs.

God said, *"Place the needs of my people upon the altar before My Presence. Jesus is praying for all their needs to be met."*

Every need, every disease, every family problem, every circumstance...God wants me to lift your need for Jesus to pray for you. Do not delay. Write all your needs on the following page and mail it to me today!

For prayer 24 hours a day, 7 days a week, call:

1-858-HELPLINE
1-858-435-7546

Brother Cerullo,

Please place these requests on the Miracle Prayer Altar and pray for these needs:

_____

_____

_____

_____

_____

❑   Enclosed is my love gift of $(£)_____ to help you win souls and to support this worldwide ministry.

❑   Please tell me how I can become a God's Victorious Army member...to help you reach the nations of the world, and receive even more anointed teaching on a monthly basis!

Name _____

Address _____

City _____ State or Province _____

Postal Code _____ Phone Number (____)_____

E-mail_____

Fax _____

Mail today to:

MORRIS CERULLO WORLD EVANGELISM

San Diego: P.O. Box 85277 • San Diego, CA 92186

Canada: P.O. Box 3600 • Concord, Ontario L4K 1B6

U.K.: P.O. Box 277 • Hemel Hempstead, Herts HP2 7DH

Web site: www.mcwe.com • **E-mail:** morriscerullo@mcwe.com

For prayer 24 hours a day, 7 days a week, call: **1-858-HELPLINE**
435-7546

HELPLINE FAX: 1-858-427-0555

HELPLINE EMAIL: helpline@mcwe.com

Miracles Happen When Someone Cares...And We Care What Happens To You!

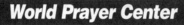

P

Call if you need healing, restoration in your marriage, financial breakthrough, deliverance from alcohol, drugs or other addictions,

R

World Prayer Center

- Prayer Help Line

- Trained, anointed intercessors. Only qualified, trained intercessors will be on the phone lines.

YOUR PHONE IS YOUR POINT OF CONTACT!

A

- Non-denominational: We encourage Catholic, Protestants, Jews, people of all faiths to call

You Never Have To Face Your Circumstances Alone!

There is no distance in prayer!

Y

Our trained intercessors are ready to pray and believe God for the miracle you need!

E

R

The New Anointing can be yours!

Yes, Brother Cerullo, I too feel the Holy Spirit moving on me to enter into a new experience of God's power in my life...and to witness answers to prayer as never before!

☐ Send me your New Anointing Prayer Cloth. (M107)

☐ Send me the New Anointing Tape Album so I can experience the anointing on this message just as you preached it. Enclosed is my love gift of $30 or more. ($45 Can., £20 U.K.) (TAO39)

☐ Enclosed is my love gift of $(£)_____ to help you win souls in the nations of the world.

Total enclosed: $(£)_____

Please pray for these needs:

_____

_____

_____

_____

_____

_____

_____

_____

_____

(Turn over)

_____

_____

_____

_____

_____

_____

_____

_____

_____

_____

_____

_____

Name: _____

Address: _____

City: _____

State or Province: _____

Postal Code: _____

MBD

Mail today to:

MORRIS CERULLO WORLD EVANGELISM

U.S.: P.O. Box 85277 • San Diego, CA 92186

U.K.: P.O. Box 277 • Hemel Hempstead HERTS HP2 7DH

CANADA: P.O. Box 3600 • Concord, Ontario L4K 1B6

Website: mcwe.com   Email: morriscerullo@mcwe.com